Teddy Bear Hamster

Teddy Bear Hamsters as pets

Teddy Bear Hamsters keeping, care, pros and cons, housing, diet and health.

by

Roger Rodendale

Table of Contents

Introduction

Of all the hamster species, the Teddy Bear Hamster, or the "Syrian Hamster", is certainly the most popular one to be kept as a pet. These little furry rodents are known for their charismatic personality. For anyone who is looking for a good pet to start off with, these are considered the best option.

Compared to the other species of hamsters, it is noted that the Teddy Bear Hamster is a lot easier to train and handle. If you have children at home, the Teddy Bear Hamster can make a wonderful pet.

Teddy Bear Hamsters are known for being extremely active and playful. Needless to say, they are also very entertaining to have around. They can get a little territorial with their own species, which makes it hard to have more than one hamster in a single cage.

Hamsters are short lived, with a life span of about 2 years at the most. As the owner, you are responsible for every day in the two years of your hamsters' lives. Now, with Teddy Bear Hamsters, you can find a great companion if you can train them well and keep them in a good condition.

Although it may seem like they are not as big a responsibility as a dog or a cat, they need the same amount of attention. It is necessary that you spend a good amount of time with your hamster everyday. They need companionship and exercise in order to be healthy.

In addition to that, you need to make sure that you are delicate with them. Handling them properly is important and you need to learn the right way to do so when you bring a hamster home. They need constant care, as they are susceptible to a lot of illnesses if they are unkempt. Regular cleaning and maintenance is a must.

You also need to be very cautious about the environment these delicate creatures are kept in. Too much noise, sudden loud sounds, smoke etc. can claim their lives in an instant.

Therefore, before you underestimate the care required for a hamster, it is necessary that you learn all you can about these creatures.

This book gives you all the information that you will need regarding feeding, maintaining and even taming your hamster. From the first day of bringing your hamster home, this book will be a useful step by step guide to raising a happy and playful furry buddy.

The information in this book is researched in great detail, providing several tips from hamster owners. Once you have gone through this book thoroughly, you will be certain if you will be able to care for a hamster or not. If you believe that you can provide a loving and conducive environment for them to thrive in, then this book will be able to help you understand the requirements of your pet and provide him with the right care.

Chapter 1: The Teddy Bear Hamster

The Teddy Bear Hamster is, undoubtedly, the most loved pet in American households, amongst others. These beautiful rodents make wonderful companions and are known for their docile behavior.

Knowing about the origin of these species and their physical description lets you know what to expect when it comes to your pet hamster. You will also understand how to identify the type of hamster that you have at home and provide specific care as required.

This chapter tells you all you need to know about the Teddy Bear Hamster so that you are well prepared to bring one of them home.

1. Origin

The book "The natural history of Aleppo" by Alexander Russell first mentioned the Teddy Bear Hamster. This was in 1797. So, quite obviously, these hamsters have been observed for a long time in their natural environment as well as in captivity.

Alexander Russell spent a good amount of time of his life in the Aleppo region in Syria as a physician. He was there for almost 10 years, starting in the year 1740. The area was swept by plague and he was the expert on this condition. While he treated cases of plague, he also made notes about the flora and fauna as well as the culture and climate of Syria. It is believed that he made the most detailed notes about life in Syria, which he published in his book.

The second edition of this book was written after his death by his nephew, Patrick Russell. It was in the second edition that the Teddy Bear Hamster or the Syrian hamster was mentioned. Although Patrick Russell is believed to have discovered this species, many claim that the unpublished pages of the first edition did contain some notes about the rodent.

In this book, the hamster has been mentioned as "less common than a field rat". A detailed description of the anatomy post the dissection of a specimen has also been mentioned in the book.

However, neither Alexander nor Patrick Russell claim that they discovered a new species of hamsters. They simply believed that the Teddy Bear Hamster was the same as a Common European hamster. They did not assign a name to the species either.

It was in the year 1839 that this hamster was presented as a whole new species by George Robert Waterhouse. He named it the Syrian Hamster. The description presented by him was based on a female specimen. He presented the new specimen to the London Zoological Society in the year 1839.

There have been several speculations that after this description of a single specimen of the Syrian hamster was presented that year, nothing was mentioned for close to 100 years. However, during the 1880s, a group of these hamsters were sent to the UK from Syria by a man named James Skeene. He was a British Counsel who took back specimens when he returned to his country from Syria.

Although Skeene himself does not mention anything in his records, there is some evidence to suggest that the Syrian Hamster was bred in Britain until the early 1900s. There is no interesting information about the species until the 1920s, however.

During that time, a parasitologist from Jerusalem, Saul Alder was studying about Leishmaniasis, which was a very prevalent disease. The Chinese Hamster was a good specimen to study as a model for this condition. However, he was not able to breed these hamsters and was also not convinced about shipping them in from China. As a result, he began to look for species that were native to his area or anywhere in the Middle East.

He read the description by Waterhouse and learnt about the Syrian hamster and wanted to obtain a few specimens for his study.

This brings us to Israel Aharoni, who was the first ever Hebrew zoologist. Basically, he was responsible for all the Hebrew names assigned to animals in that area.

He is known for conducting expeditions across Jerusalem, which was then ruled by the Turks. He was the only Jew of that time who had acquired protection from the Turkish Sultan in order to carry out his travels. This was primarily because he had obtained rare species of butterflies for the

Sultan's collection. It is believed that during these collection expeditions, he had brought home any species of animal that he thought of as unusual. Most of them were sent away to Berlin and some remained in the Hebrew University of Jerusalem. In the year 1930, when Saul Alder was on the lookout for local species of hamsters, it was Aharoni who was put on the job.

He wrote about the kind of hamster he was looking for in quite some detail in his memoirs. However, there is very little evidence to suggest whether he actually ever found a specimen or not.

When he arrived in Aleppo, he requested a local guide in Syria to seek information about the species of hamster from a Sheik who owned a certain farm. The sheik obliged by calling a meeting and began to search for the species in one of his best farms. It was believed that a colony had been spotted there.

The farm area was dug up thoroughly and after practically destroying all the crops, a nest with one female and 11 hamster pups was unearthed. They were all placed in a box, assuming that the mother would take care of them. However, when the Syrian guide saw that the mother hamster actually killed one of her babies. That left Aharoni with 10 Teddy Bear Hamster pups to take care of.

He fostered them until there was an escape from the cage. They were only able to trace 9 of them, which were then taken to the Hebrew University Animal Facility to put them under the care of Hein Ben-Menchen, the founder.

These 9 specimens were kept in a wooden cage. Sadly, they escaped by chewing their way out. Only four were found after this escape. It consisted of one female and three males. Some researchers say that it was vice versa with one male and three females. It was also believed that of the three females, one was killed by a male. This was the first time that the Syrian hamster was bred in captivity.

After the first batch was bred, they were handed over to the publisher of the first ever report on the research conducted on these Syrian hamsters, Alder. These colonies were further distributed to other laboratories across the globe for research.

It was in the year 1931 that the first batch of these hamsters was brought to England. They were actually smuggled into the country.

Most records that are available show that these hamsters arrived in the United States seven years after. The next mentioned record of hamsters in the United States is only in the year 1971. A group of 12 Syrian hamsters that were captured in the wild were taken back to the USA.

Their value as household pets became known during this time, as the records state that with 3 days of handling and caring, they became extremely tame. Within four weeks the specimens mated to produce litters. Each litter consisted of 11 puppies on average and they were all raised and weaned.

It is interesting to note that several attempts were made to capture wild Syrian hamsters and bring them back to the United States. Yet, in every case, there were escapes that led to them going back into the wild. These rodents were extremely hard to capture after they had managed to break out of their enclosures.

One such example is that of Bill Duncan, who captured two females in the same area in Aleppo. This group disappeared without any trace.

Then two years after, a Rodent Control Officer was able to capture two more specimens. This time they consumed rat bait and died immediately. The same officer captured a pair of Syrian hamsters. While the male died, the female was taken to England into quarantine. However, no breeding efforts were made with her.

The most important thing to note about Syrian Hamsters is that they are considered rare only because their natural range is very limited. However, given the natural range, these hamsters have always been found in considerably large numbers.

Today, these hamsters are bred world over and are the most popular type of hamster.

2. Description

Of all the varieties of hamsters that are preferred as pets, the Teddy Bear Hamster is the largest. When you are buying a Teddy Bear Hamster, remember that this is a name commonly associated with certain varieties of the Syrian hamster that are longhaired. You have other names like the black bear hamster that are popular in the market, too. They simply denote the coat coloration or type and not an entire species by themselves. All these varieties of hamsters are scientifically categorized as *Mesocriceus auratus.*

These hamsters are usually close to 13cms or about 5.5 inches in length. They are known to get larger in some cases. In fact, the female Syrian hamsters are always larger than the males.

These hamsters are extremely stocky and have large eyes. The tulip-shaped ears are a characteristic trait of these hamsters. The tail is usually short. They are known as the "golden hamsters" because of the wild coloration of the animal, which is brown for the most part. They have black ticks on the upper part of the body. This covers two thirds of the coat of the hamster. The fur on the belly is generally white with an undercoat that is grey in color.

The tail of these hamsters is pretty short, often difficult to see. It measures at about $1/6^{th}$ of the total length of the animal's body. The most incredible characteristic of a Syrian hamster, or any species of hamster, is their incisors. The upper and lower pair of incisors keep growing all their lives. They wear them down by chewing. Therefore, you need to make sure that you provide your pet with enough toys.

The bones of hamsters are very fragile. Their body is extremely flexible. In addition to this, these creatures are sensitive to any changes in temperature. They cannot withstand drafts, sudden changes in temperature from hot to cold and vice versa.

Flashes of black are also seen on the cheeks of these hamsters. One interesting characteristic of Syrian hamsters is the cheek pouch. These pouches are meant to carry food back to the burrow. They are able to store large amounts of food in them.

The sensory system of hamsters is worth noting. They have very poor eyesight and are known to be shortsighted. Hamsters are also completely color blind.

However, they have special scent glands that help the rodent find its way around. Whenever they walk across an object and rub against some substrate, they leave a trail of scent. This scent helps them distinguish between a male and a female and also allows them to look for food in the wild.

The scent glands are known as "hip spots" that are seen on each hip. This also helps them mark their territory. In fact, the ability to mark territory with strong scents makes these hamsters extremely territorial and aggressive.

The scent glands in the Syrian hamsters are also used to alert the opposite gender for mating. It produces a sticky substance that causes the scent. This is prominently seen in males. The females use their scent glands to lure a male into the burrow when they are ready for mating.

They have a very sharp sense of hearing. It makes them extremely sensitive to sounds that are very high pitched. The communication of a hamster is usually in the ultrasonic sound range.

There are several mutations that have taken place over the years of captive breeding of these hamsters. There are various coat types and textures that you will have to know about in order to identify the right type of hamster to bring home.

3. Different varieties

There are several varieties, over 40 colorations, in fact. Primarily, they are separated into shorthaired, longhaired and rex hamsters.

a. Length of hair

The longhaired varieties: these are referred to as the Teddy Bear Hamsters locally. The hair in males is longer than that of the females. In some cases, the females may look like any other shorthaired hamster.

The shorthaired varieties: they have short fur and are usually referred to as "Fancy" hamsters/

Rex Hamsters: these hamsters are the most rare of all Syrian hamsters. They have a puffy appearance and it almost seems like their hair is being lifted because of the guard hair below, which is much shorter. The whiskers in this variety are curly.

All three varieties are available in the Satin type, which is a certain gene that makes the skin look extremely glossy. This is primarily because the hair of hamsters with this gene is thinner and there are fewer cells that are filled with air. That makes the surface reflective.

b. Markings and patterns

There are three markings that are commonly found. Of these, the banded and dominant spot varieties are the most prominent ones. The three patterns that you can expect with Teddy Bear Hamsters are:

- Banded: These hamsters have a white color band that will run around the center of the body. This band should be about $1/3^{rd}$ of the length of the whole body for the hamster to qualify for showing. The belly fur in these varieties is usually white. The hard part about banded hamsters is breeding them. They will have intermingled colors in the band, which makes it harder to get the exact banded variety that you want.

- Dominant spot: The name implies that these hamsters have spots on their fur. These spots are usually seen on the back and on the whole face. There is a blaze, which is quite noticeable on the forehead of the hamster.

- Piebald: This is one of the earliest spotting genes that was seen in Syrian hamsters. It is also known as irregular spotting. Sometimes, the patterns also resemble brindled fur. But for the most part, the pattern on the fur is very haphazard.

c. Genetic modifications

Syrian hamsters carry certain genes that can lead to certain diseases or even peculiar coat colorations. Here are a few genes that every hamster owner should know about:

- **Lethal and Semi Lethal:** These genes are the result of a mutation that doubles a certain gene in the hamster. This usually leads to the death of the hamsters. Pet owners will usually encounter these genes with dominant spot varieties or light grey varieties. The other lethal genes are restricted to laboratories and are seldom circulated among those who want to bring home hamsters as pets. If two hamsters carrying these genes are bred, a major portion of the litter will die before they are delivered. In this case, the dead embryos are absorbed by the body of the mother hamster. If that fails, the mother will die too. If any of the puppies survive, they may not carry the gene necessarily.

- **Anopthalmic whites:** These hamsters usually carry a semi lethal gene. They are also referred to as the blind white or the eyeless white. Usually these genes are found in hamsters like the Roan or the Black Eyed white varieties that have white bellies. If two hamsters carrying these genes are mated, a quarter of the resulting litter will be eyeless. The term eyeless signifies that the eyes will actually not be existent or may not be functional.

A good knowledge of mutations is necessary to help you pick the right coat colors that are less likely to carry a certain mutation. The most commonly available colors with Teddy Bear Hamsters are Golden, Cream, Cinnamon, White, Black, Sable and Silver Grey.

4. Personality of Teddy Bear Hamsters

Teddy Bear Hamsters are the best option for a household with children, as they are easier to tame. In addition to that, these hamsters are larger and easier to handle. But remember never to leave a child unsupervised with a hamster, as they have really sharp teeth. It is best that you ensure that your child is at least 10 years of age or older.

The most important thing to know about Teddy Bear Hamsters is that they will not give you the same devotion as a dog. However, they like interacting with human beings and need your attention to some extent in order to stay mentally active.

a. Great energy
Teddy Bear Hamsters are a big bundle of energy. This is because in the wild they will walk for hours and travel far and wide looking for food. Essentially, movement and exercise is second nature to them. They have the ability to store energy and make use of it when they have bursts of activity.

This is one of the reasons why it is very important for you to have a hamster wheel in your pet's enclosure. You will notice that they will run up to five miles every single day. The ability to store food makes them a lot more able to do stay this active. They will also stay asleep for long hours during the day so that they can gear up for nighttime when the activity actually begins.

b. Docile
If your interactions with your hamster are regular and you get them used to being handled, you can have a great companion. Hamsters love being with their owners, albeit not as much as a pet like the dog. They are extremely easy to tame. In the case of the Syrian hamster especially, you will notice that it takes a lot less time to get them tame enough to live in your household.

It is this temperament that actually makes them so popular as pets. They will seldom attack their owners or get aggressive even during the breeding period.

That said, you must not expect the Teddy Bear Hamster to immediately love cuddling with you and being petted. They take some taming and some time to get used to all the petting and affection. It is also a good idea to talk to your hamster just before you go to bed, as it is possibly the only time you will have to interact with these nocturnal rodents properly.

c. Territorial
As discussed, Teddy Bear Hamsters mark their territories with their scent glands. These strong scents make them extremely territorial and almost intolerant towards other hamsters. Now, if you have two children at home, getting each a hamster of their own is a good idea. That is, only if you are willing to keep them in separate cages and give them entirely different supplies.

Hamsters of the same gender are very aggressive towards each other. They can cause serious damage and even kill another hamster in some cases. The only time when these hamsters are able to live in the same territory is when they are in heat. Then you can keep a male and a female in one cage. However, after the mating season is over, they will not want to have anything to do with one another and may get into serious fights.

d. Best housekeepers

Teddy Bear Hamsters really love to keep their space in great shape. They cannot tolerate any mess within the space that they live in. In fact, younger hamsters will make sure that they get their food away from the nesting area as well as the area that they urinate or poop in.

Only when they are older, the food is soaked in urine to make sure that the fragile teeth are able to chew through it.

In addition to all of this, they also love to keep their housing area clean. They will occasionally dig through the substrate and fling out any debris, pieces of rotting food, broken toys etc.

e. Easily startled

The one thing you need to be careful not to do is to startle your hamster. When they are asleep, it is best that you let them do so without any disturbances. If you wake them up, you must be prepared for a bite.

Any sudden movement or jarring sound can make them very skittish and startled. This is why it is necessary to keep your Teddy Bear Hamster away from areas like the television room if you want to promote better health in your pet.

These nocturnal creatures certainly make great pets. However, you need to remember that the responsibility of having a Teddy Bear Hamster should never be taken lightly.

In the following chapters we will discuss everything you need to be prepared for when you bring a Teddy Bear Hamster home. Only when you are entirely certain of being able to provide all the care requirements should you bring one home.

Chapter 2: Before the hamster comes home

Rethinking the responsibility of buying a hamster, researching about the best options available to you to get a healthy hamster and knowing how to choose a healthy hamster is necessary information for any potential hamster owner.

1. Considerations before buying a hamster

As we discussed before, a hamster typically lives for about 2 years, sometimes longer. You need to commit to your pet and make sure that you are ready to spend some time caring for him.

Now, relatively, these creatures are easy to take care of. As for children over the age of 10, they do make good pets. If you are solely bringing a Teddy Bear Hamster home to make your child more responsible, it is important to have at least one adult member from the household who will share the responsibility.

Hamsters are susceptible to illnesses and may require additional care. It is possible that they get injured or need medical attention. This can be pretty expensive. In addition to that, you need to make sure that you take your pet for regular vet visits. If there are wounds, be prepared to clean them, administer medicines and take good care of the hamster.

When you bring a hamster home, you need to make sure you take care of the following:

- Daily feeding
- Daily change of water in the bottle
- Daily interaction
- Weekly cleaning of the cage.

You also have to think about things like where you will place the cage in the house to ensure that the hamster is completely safe. You must also consider your own schedule. If you are a frequent traveler, you need to make arrangements for your pet to be taken care of while you are away. You may have to board your hamster at a pet hostel or you could hire a pet sitter to take care of the hamster. This, again, is an additional cost.

Your hamster is nocturnal. Therefore, you should be able to stay up for at least an hour after 8 pm. Essentially, your hamster will be asleep all day and will be active after 8 pm. That is the time you have to dedicate for interactions with your pet. Not being able to do this will turn your hamster into a lethargic and unfriendly pet. Then, you also put yourself at risk of being bitten or attacked.

The other thing you need to understand is that the housing area of the hamster is going to be noisy. The wheel and the scurrying about will seem like a din when you are trying to get some sleep. If that bothers you, you must be prepared to at least give your pet a separate room or keep him in a safe place where the noise is not too audible.

Besides these things, a major consideration is the cost of owning a hamster. It is necessary for you to set aside a hamster fund if you want to be a good pet parent.

2. Costs of keeping a Teddy Bear Hamster

A Teddy Bear Hamster has certain requirements that you just cannot ignore. The costs of owning a hamster will mostly include the following:

When you buy a hamster you will need to get a lot of equipment such as the food dish, the water dish, toys, equipment for exercise and a lot more. On average, a good-sized cage or enclosure for your hamster should cost $60-150 or £30-£100. It depends on the size of the cage and the material it is made of. Ideally, you should get the largest cage you can in your budget. You also have to set up the cage with accessories that may cost $20-60 or £10-30.

Food is a constant expenditure. The quality of food is something you cannot compromise on. Your hamster will need dried pellets, grains and assorted vegetables. The quantity of food is, no doubt, not very high. You can expect an expenditure of about $5-10 or £2-8 every month. This can vary depending upon the size of your hamster and the special conditions, such as the breeding season, when your pet would require more food.

Bedding is essential for your hamster to be cozy. The need to burrow and dig is also satisfied when you give the hamster a good substrate material. You need to cover the floor entirely to also make sure that the cage can be maintained well. Good quality material will cost you between $5-10 or £2-8 each month. This depends on the size of your cage and how frequently you prefer to change the substrate of the cage. If you clean it on a daily basis, the budget will be a lot higher.

It is mandatory to have a vet fund for your pet. Since hamsters are hard to insure, it is advisable to set aside some money each month for the medical expenses of your pet.

You cannot ignore the miscellaneous costs associated with your pet. You may have unexpected accidents or injuries that need medical attention. In addition to that, you may want to indulge your pet from time to time and get him a few toys and accessories. Have an additional $10 or £5 set aside for emergencies.

On average, you can expect close to $400 or £225 per year to make sure that your hamster is completely comfortable. You need to be honest about the availability of these funds. Even if it seems like a small amount, it can seem like a stretch if you do not have enough to run your home comfortably.

Once you have made the commitment, you will have to stick by it for at least 2 years, or your furry friend may end up in a rescue shelter or develop behavioral issues. Once you have put all the considerations into perspective, you can be certain that you are ready to become a good parent to a cuddly little Teddy Bear Hamster

3. 10 reasons hamsters are wonderful pets

There is a big responsibility associated with hamsters, no doubt. But, if you decide to open your hearts to them, you can be assured of two or three years of great companionship and of course loads of entertainment. Here are 10 reasons why a hamster is a great pet to have:

1. They are cuddly and warm

When it comes to smaller pets, hamsters are the best option because they are just so adorable and cute. These furry creatures like to spend time with their pet owners. There is absolutely no doubt that they make the most wonderful furry companions.

2. Breeding as a hobby

Several hamster owners choose breeding as a hobby. This is because hamsters will breed quite often, usually about 4 times a year. There are several characteristics like the coats and the temperament of each litter that breeders can work on. It is a great sense of accomplishment to achieve what you put your mind to when it comes to each breeding season. You will have a lot of fun with it and will also meet new people and make good friends in the process of meeting experienced breeders.

3. They do not smell bad

Having a pet at home usually means having that constant odor in your home. However, hamsters are extremely clean creatures that will make all the effort to keep their cage clean. In addition to that, the plus side is that they are naturally odorless. They will also have specific urine spots that can be cleaned on a daily basis. If you do that, you will not have to worry about any odor.

4. Guests are comfortable

Sometimes a pet like a dog can get really intimidating for a guest. They tend to get territorial or extremely excited. It makes them either bark at the guests or jumpy. Not everyone is comfortable with this.

Now, with hamsters, they are usually not even noticed. Even when they are, they are not intimidating. Although it is not advised that you let people touch and pick up your hamster before he is fully trained, you will not have to worry about your guests, even kids, getting scared or being uncomfortable in the presence of the hamster.

5. They don't take up too much space

It is really unfair to have larger pets in a place that is small. But, if you really want to have a pet and need the companionship of one, a hamster is the best option possible. They will just need a few feet for the cage and the supplies. So, for those who are living in a small apartment or a dormitory, they make the best pets. In places like New York where the apartments are usually small, they make the best and most wonderful pets.

6. You don't have to worry about the entertainment

Most pets require you to spend a lot of time exercising them or playing with them. When the weather is dull or if you have had a bad day, you may just not want to do that.

With hamsters, spending about 30 minutes bonding with him is good enough. Normally, a hamster will get busy with their own cleaning up of the cage, running on the wheel or just burrowing in the substrate and do not need constant attention. That lets you stay guilt free even when you are not really up for an hour's play with your pet.

7. They are low maintenance

You do not have to work too hard to raise a hamster. Besides the fact that they entertain themselves for the most part, you don't even have to feel guilty about leaving them home while you are at work. They usually sleep all day and will wake up only at night. You can keep your hamster happy, healthy and safe without too much work, making them the perfect pet if you have a rather busy schedule.

8. They are entertaining

Watching your hamster scurrying about in the cage and being so busy all the time is rather entertaining. You will never feel bored for a minute after they are awake. In addition to that, the Teddy Bear Hamster has the trademark chubby cheeks and pointy ears that you can keep looking at all day. They often make silly faces that are very endearing.

9. They are more affordable

In comparison to pets like dogs or cats, hamsters are a smarter choice if you are looking at the financial side of it. They are cheap to buy and will not need as much each month as a dog or a cat.

10. They are great companions

The ultimate goal of getting a pet is companionship. You can certainly not train a hamster to perform a lot of tricks for you, of course. But watching them can be very exciting and entertaining. Once you have earned their trust, they don't mind sitting on your lap, being around you while you read a book or even cuddle up with you when you are watching a movie.

In general, hamsters make great pets if you are willing to put up with a few issues mentioned above. For the most part, they are the easier and the more practical option for working professionals or for people who are studying.

4. Choosing your hamster

Deciding which type of hamster you want to buy is the first step. If you are reading this book, then it is certain that you have set your mind on the Teddy Bear Hamster. These are considered to be among the best of all the breeds available, as they are playful and much easier to handle. However, when you are choosing a hamster for yourself, here are a few things that you will have to consider to ensure that you have a pet that is suitable for the environment in your home.

What gender is preferable?

With any type of Syrian Hamster, especially the Teddy Bear Hamster, it is best that you consider the gender that you pick, as they will have very unique temperaments. The female is a lot more aggressive than the male, especially during the breeding season. On the other hand, some breeders may warn you of the placid nature of a male hamster. However, this really depends upon the personality of the hamster that you choose. Now, the only thing you need to make sure of is that when you choose a female, she has been separated from male hamsters, or at least make sure that she is not expecting a litter.

Find a hamster that is easy to handle

No matter where you decide to buy your hamster from, make sure you interact with them before you bring them home. Don't be afraid to handle the hamster. If they are unsocial, you will know as soon as you approach them. A tame hamster is calm when you try to handle him. He will just sniff around for food and will be comfortable in your hands. He should be curious and should be interested in interacting with you. That is a sign that the hamster is calm and relaxed. If you see that he is jittery and uncomfortable, you may want to move on to another one.

The hamster should be healthy

Making sure that your hamster is healthy is really important. If you do bring a hamster home that is unwell and you do not take the necessary measures to nurse him back to health, it could be fatal for him. Any hamster that is poorly maintained is likely to succumb in a new environment, even when you try your best to keep him in good condition.

Here are the signs of good health in a Teddy Bear Hamster:

- The eyes, mouth and nose are clear
- The coat is shiny
- The gait is steady
- The nose is not runny
- There are no lumps on the body
- He does not have any hair loss
- There are no overgrown teeth

You have several other minor criterion such as the coat color that you can choose from. But the most important thing is to find a hamster that is used to human interaction and one that is not likely to develop any health issues. The next step is to figure out where to get your hamster from.

5. Where to buy a hamster

If you have decided to bring home a hamster, the next question is where to buy one from. There are several options that you can choose from based on your convenience.

There are several breeders or pet stores that you can purchase a hamster from. You also have the option of being a foster parent or adopting a hamster from a shelter.

In this chapter, we will discuss all the pros and cons of getting a hamster from various sources. You need to make sure that whatever choice you make, the pet that you will bring home is healthy and in good condition.

a. Buying from a breeder
Usually hamster owners tend to breed them on their own. It is a very popular hobby among hamster owners. Most hamster owners breed their pets in order to get new coat colors or to breed puppies that can win hamster shows.

In addition to that, you also have the option of buying from hamster owners. They may have had a litter that they are unable to take care of. When you buy a hamster from a hobbyist, you have the advantage of bringing home a pet that is healthy and also used to being handled quite regularly.

When you approach a show breeder, you can expect the breeding to be very well planned. The puppies are produced in such a way that they are healthy, of good temperament and also robust. You can talk to hamster owners or even approach local hamster clubs to find out about these private hamster owners.

When you buy from a breeder or a hobbyist, you have the advantage of knowing the parents of your hamsters. That means you are aware of any genetic conditions or diseases that the parent hamsters may have had. You will also be sure of the age of your hamster.

b. Buying from a pet shop
Personally, getting any pet from a pet store is never the best idea unless it is your last option. The issue with most of these pet stores is that the hamsters are obtained from a commercial breeder. They are bred on farms in large masses. This means that they have not been handled by humans and also they may not be in the best condition. The most human handling that they get is when any staff from the pet shop is trying to make a sale.

However, if you do decide to buy a hamster from a pet shop, make sure that they have been quarantined before they are put up for sale. This reduces any chances of diseases from existing pets and also ensures that the exiting hamsters have not contracted any condition thanks to the new arrivals.

You must also make it a point to ask for an assessment of the health and temperament of each hamster. They must be checked by a vet and should be declared free from genetic conditions. Unlike a pet like a dog, you will not have to worry about dealing with diseases on a long term basis. Nevertheless, the last thing you want is to see is a pet, even if he is only going to be around for about three years, suffers from diseases that cannot be controlled.

If this is your second hamster in your home, make sure that you only bring him home from a reliable source. Otherwise, your current pet may develop health issues. In addition to that, human beings are susceptible to several health disorders due to regular handling of a hamster. Only make purchases from reliable and recommended pet stores.

c. Rescue shelters
There are several cases of abandoned hamsters. They are left at rescue shelters because the owners had to move homes, their children were unable to get along with the pet, they were unable to afford it and many other reasons.

It is a wonderful idea to bring home a hamster that was abandoned. Most hamsters that end up in a rescue shelter are completely assessed on their health. They are also given the treatment that they require before they are rehomed. In rescue homes with several volunteers, you can also expect the animal to be handled well, therefore guaranteeing good temperament.

However, if you are bringing a hamster home from a rescue shelter, you can never be sure of his background. Of course, age is another factor that you cannot be sure of. In most cases, the health assessment will give you an approximation of the age of the hamster that you have brought home.

The process of adopting a hamster depends upon the recue shelter that you are going to approach. There are several forms that you will have to fill out. In addition to that, you can also expect a home visit and a background check from the volunteers.

This is primarily to ensure that the hamster is going to a good home where he will be loved and cared for. Once you have cleared all the checks for adoption, you will be ready to bring home your new hamster. Some rescue shelters may charge you a small adoption fee that will cover the medical expenses of the hamster while in their care. In most cases, you will not have to pay anything to bring your hamster home.

d. Making sure your source is reliable
When you decide to buy from a pet store or a breeder, make sure that you are sure that your source is reliable. This means that they should be genuinely concerned with raising healthy and happy animals for sale. If not, you are not only going to bring home a hamster who is possibly unwell and you are also encouraging a cruel commercial practice that often thrives at the expense of these beautiful creatures.

You can do this check yourself with a few simple things that you should observe when you approach a pet store or a breeder:

- Always choose a smaller but recommended pet store or breeder over a large chain or breeding farm. When the source is smaller, you know that the hamsters will be given a lot of personal attention. This means that the breeder or the pet store staff will spend quality time with them and will make them ready to be sold in terms of their health and tameness.

- Inspect the cage or the enclosure that they have been kept in. The hamsters should have complete access to fresh food and water. The bedding should be clean and there must be accessories like the wheel that will provide exercise for the hamsters.

- Ideally, Syrian hamsters will not be kept in pairs or large numbers. This is because of their inherent territorial nature. However, if you do see groups of hamsters in a cage, they are probably very young. They should display no aggression towards one another and should be active when awake. If you see that one or more of them are retreating to a corner of the cage, it could be an indication of behavioral issues.

- The hamster should look healthy. The mark of a hamster that is being fed on time is a shiny coat and beady bright eyes. This shows that they have also been given ample exercise.

- Ask questions. Make sure that the breeder or the pet store staff knows how to handle hamsters. You can ask them about the food that is given to these hamsters, the behavior, the number of times they are brought out of the cage, etc.

- Make sure you ask for references from their customers. If the pet store or breeder is hesitant to connect you with previous customers, it is a sign of caution. If they are readily providing you with references, you can be assured that they have nothing that they do not want to disclose.

- Ask them for a health certificate. This will tell you about the genetic condition, the history and the general health of the hamster that you are going to bring home. All good pet stores and breeders will be able to give you a health certificate. However, the lack of this facility is not a clear indication that they are a bad source to obtain a hamster from.

When you are buying your hamster, work with your instinct. If you feel, at any point, that you are being taken for a ride, just move on to the next store or breeder that you know.

e. Consider fostering
If this is your first time with a hamster, consider fostering the pet of a friend or relative. This is great insight to tell you whether you are really ready for a pet or not.

You will get first-hand experience with what it takes to keep a hamster healthy. You will also know whether the nocturnal habits of the hamster will bother you. The most important thing is that you will know if your new pet will interfere with your schedule. If that happens, you can try to work your schedule accordingly or make the right choice about bringing a hamster home. The most important revelation with fostering a pet is whether you are financially ready for this commitment.

If you feel overwhelmed with a pet you do not have to worry about it or feel guilty, as he will go back home to his owners. On the other hand, if you are certain that you like the experience, you will be ready to open your home to a loving and furry Teddy Bear Hamster.

Once you have brought a pet home, the next step is to make your home ready for him to be comfortable and happy in.

6. Housing the hamster

Before you bring the hamster home, you need to make sure that he has a housing area that is designated to him. The cage is the most important item that you will be investing in when you buy a hamster. So, make sure that you think about all the options that you have and invest carefully.

You need to think about the safety, maintenance, size and the budget that you have. Remember that when you are bringing a Teddy Bear Hamster home, you can only keep one in each enclosure because they are extremely territorial.

a. How big should the cage be?
The burrows that hamsters make in the wild are very organized. They have a separate area that they eat in, they make a chamber to sleep in and also have a defined place to eliminate waste in. That is the precise luxury that your pet will expect even in a cage. It is instinctive for a hamster to designate a space for everything in their homes, just as we humans do.

So, it is quite obvious that they will need a cage that is large enough for these separations.

If your pet has a very small and cramped cage, he will be chronically stressed. The rule with cages is that the larger the enclosure, the better. They will need a minimum of 10,000 cm^2 of space. When he stands up or rears up on the hind legs, there should be a clearance of at least 6 inches above his head. If your hamster is in a very small space, chances are that he will show signs of boredom. Incessant chewing on the cage bars is a sure shot sign that your hamster is bored

You must also consider the space needed for your hamster to nest in case you decide to breed. They also need to be able to burrow, which means that the height of the cage should be good enough.

b. What are the types of cages?
With hamster cages, you have four basic options. We will discuss the advantages and the disadvantages of each in this section. You will also learn about choosing the right type of cage for your Teddy Bear Hamster.

Wired cages:

This is one of the most popular types of cages. You will have a wire cage that is powder coated with a plastic base that is detachable. One interesting feature is that you can get various levels that the hamster can walk around in and explore. However, avoid getting a cage that is too tall, as it can be dangerous for your Teddy Bear Hamster, which does not have good depth perception. That means that he may fall from one of the higher platforms, leading to serious injuries.

Required size: It is good to buy a cage that is at least two square feet in floor area.

How to choose one: Make sure that the distance between the bars is less than half an inch. This will make sure that your hamster is not able to squeeze his way through. The rule is that if the head can go through, the body will too.

You will have to add a cardboard platform, some ceramic tile or mat on the floor of the cage. The wire can be very uncomfortable for the tiny paws of your Teddy Bear Hamster.

A wire cage will cost you a little over $35 or £15. The cost entirely depends on the size of the cage that you want to buy for your hamster.

Advantages: The best thing about wired cages is that

• They provide good ventilation
• They are entertaining for your hamster thanks to the different levels.

- You can get a whole range of styles with these cages.

Disadvantages: The concerns with respect to the wired cages are:
- The chances of your hamster escaping are quite high even if there is the slightest gap in the bars.
- If you have other pets like cats or dogs, there are chances that they can get their paws into the cage and hurt the hamster.
- Kids can get their hands into the cage and can get bitten.

Aquarium

An aquarium is basically an enclosure that is either made of solid glass or some form of plexi glass. This type of housing arrangement usually does not have any cover on the top, which requires you to place some mesh there. Otherwise you will notice that your hamster will be gone in the dead of the night.

You will not find aquariums that are specially designed for hamsters. However, you can buy one from the section designated to fish and the other aquatic section of any store.

In the case of an aquarium you have to be extra careful about keeping it completely clean for your hamster. Since the ventilation is not that great, you will see that most odors are trapped inside the aquarium. This will make your hamster feel really uncomfortable and will reduce the quality of his life drastically.

It does not matter if the aquarium itself looks very clean. The problem is the bedding material that will absorb the water and urine, making it smell bad. You will have to clean the cage every week or as frequently as needed.

Required size: You need to have an aquarium that is it least 24 inches in length and about 12 inches in width. A 10 gallon aquarium can be very small for a Teddy Bear Hamster. You should look for an aquarium that is longer and not for one that is taller.

How to choose one: You need to find a cover that fits well and has a mesh that is durable. A hamster can chew through the wired mesh in no time if it isn't of premium quality.

You will spend about $45 or £20 on an aquarium that is about 20 gallons in size. The mesh will have to be bought separately.

Advantages:
You will find the aquarium extremely useful in:
- Keeping the hamster from escaping
- Preventing any pet or child from getting too close to the hamster.
- You can view the activity of the hamster easily thanks to the transparent sides.

Disadvantages:
- They need a lot more maintenance than a wired cage.
- Ventilation inside the aquarium is quite poor.
- It is a very boring set up for a hamster and will require you to add a lot of entertainment to make sure that he is happy.

Cage and aquarium combination
If you are not sure if a cage works for your hamster or whether you should choose an aquarium, you can try a combination. That way, you will be able to get an enclosure that gives your pet ample space and at the same time, you will also have the safety that your hamster needs.

With these combination aquariums, you will get a wired cage that you can attach on top. That way your hamster will get a sort of duplex that he can live in and play in.

Advantages:
- There is ample ventilation thanks to the upper wired area
- It gives your hamster a lot of opportunity to get good exercise, as he can climb up and down.
- You have ample space in the base for your hamster to nest, burrow and simply dig around.
- It is more spacious than any other kind of hamster enclosure.

Disadvantages:
- It can be quite a stretch to take off the wired upper area every time you decide to clean the aquarium.
- This is a lot more expensive than the other kinds of enclosures that you will find in most pet stores.

Plastic habitats
These beautiful enclosures are also known as modular hamster cages. They are beautiful to look at and have been marketed quite widely for being the ideal type of enclosure for a hamster.

However, most enthusiasts have shunned these cages because they do not provide the best ventilation for your hamster. They are also quite hard to clean.

Some of these habitats have been tweaked to include a section of wire sliding that will provide your hamster with the ventilation that he requires.

Required size: The base unit in these enclosures is usually smaller. However, there are several sections that you can extend either vertically or horizontally. This makes it possible for the hamster to get the exercise that he needs. However, you have a very small range of sizes with these modular enclosures. You will see that they cannot really match up to the size of the aquariums and cages.

You will end up spending between $40-65 or about £20-30 on the larger modular cages. However, they can be really small if you try to compromise on the cost.

In any case, this is the least recommended type of enclosure for a Teddy Bear Hamster. The tubing in these cages can be risky, as they tend to trap a hamster as large as the Teddy Bear Hamster.

Advantages:
• They are extremely solid in their construction.
• You can be sure that kids and pets will not be able to bother the hamster and also stay safe themselves.
• You can expand it as you like thanks to the flexible design.
• There are tunnels and levels that are fun for the hamster to explore and play in.

Disadvantages:
• The ventilation is quite poor, making it susceptible to odors and harder to clean.
• There are several nooks and crannies that become sites that harbor bacteria.
• A larger hamster will get stuck in the tubes, making it dangerous.
• The nests, when made inside the tunnel, can make it harder for you to take care of the puppies.

Make sure that you look for an enclosure that will conveniently fit into your home and the space available. The budget is one very important consideration. However, since it is a one-time investment, you must try not to make any compromises.

c. Where do you place the cage?
Once you have decided what type of cage you want for your hamster, the next step is to figure out where you will keep it. Here are some tips to make sure that the enclosure is in a place that is comfortable for your hamster:

- The temperature required for a hamster to thrive is about 65 degrees F, so you need to keep the cage away from any heat source that is very strong. This includes stoves, fireplaces and even windows with direct sunlight. If your hamster is in an aquarium or a modular cage that does not have ample ventilation, it can heat up even faster.

- Nevertheless, do not put your hamster in a room where there is no heat at all, such as the garage. If the temperature falls much below 65 degrees, your hamster will become extra active to keep himself warm. At temperatures around 50 degrees, your hamster will be prompted to hibernate.

- There should not be any drafts in the area where the cage has been placed. This includes doors, windows or any place that is too elevated.

- If you sleep very lightly, you should not keep the cage in your room, as the hamster will get noisy at night.

- The kitchen is the worst place to keep the cage in. Firstly, it can provide sources of a lot of heat. Secondly, your hamster will regularly kick bedding out of the cage, which can contaminate your food or areas of preparation accidentally.

- The cages should be in an area that is away from pets like dogs or cats.

- If you have younger children at home, make sure that the cage is well out of their reach. You should be able to control the interaction between the hamster and the child.

d. Accessories for the cage
Just buying a cage is not good enough; you need to make sure that it is good enough for your hamster to stay in. That means it needs to be comfortable, practical and most importantly, entertaining. That is possible only when you have the right accessories in your hamster's cage. Here are the accessories that you will need for your hamster cage:

- A hamster wheel: You will need a good enough wheel to provide your hamster with the exercise that he needs. For a large hamster like the Teddy Bear Hamster, you will need a 12 inch wheel. This is also called a Flying Saucer wheel. Barred wheels and wheels with a mesh are a complete no-no. This puts them at the risk of trapping their limbs or even developing bumble foot.

  You will know that the wheel is small for your hamster when he has an arched back while running.

- Food bowls and a water bottle: A bottle is best recommended for a hamster, as there are no chances of it toppling over. Just make sure that it doesn't leak. If the bottle leaves the bedding all moist, it will lead to bacterial growth.

  You will be advised to scatter feed your hamster. But for a Teddy Bear Hamster, this is not the best idea. Instead, get him a food bowl. That will help you keep track of how much your hamster is eating. Don't get a bowl that will occupy a lot of space in the cage, as your hamster will feel crammed.

  You get special log bridges that you can place over the bowl. This will prevent your hamster from digging into the bowl and will also prevent any wood shavings from getting into the food bowl.

- Substrate: The lining or the substrate is very important to maintain the hygiene of your hamster cage. There are several options such as saw dust and wood shavings. However, cedar and pine should be avoided, as it leads to respiratory diseases in your hamster.

  Some people even use paper shreds as substrate. You can opt for readymade substrate like Carefresh. Whatever you choose, make sure it is absorbent and easy for the hamster to dig through.

  You will need to have about 3 inches of substrate. It is best that you clean it on a regular basis. If not, your hamster will do the deed and just throw out the dirty substrate.

  The substrate should be placed in one corner of the hamster cage. You must also have ample substrate in your home to replace in the cage regularly. Whenever you see that it is soiled or wet, scoop it out and replace it. This will help your hamster also feel a lot more comfortable in his own space.

- Bedding: As mentioned before, your hamster will need a separate sleeping area. You must not get any material that will break into strands. This will make them develop digestive issues upon consuming. The material that you must avoid is cotton wool or anything fluffy. These materials will also get your hamster's limbs entangled.

  Instinctively, hamsters tend to dislocate their own limbs in order to escape any entanglement. In some worst case scenarios, they have even chewed on their limbs in a desperate attempt to untangle themselves.

  The best option is to use shredded paper as bedding for your hamster. You will also get bedding that is branded and made especially for hamsters. You will be able to get pre-ripped tissue in pet stores.

- Toys: Making the hamster cage a stimulating environment for your hamster is a must. This is possible with toys. You need to get as many toys as you can. The hamster should be able to climb, run, hide and even forage in his cage. You will get ample toys that are meant for this.

  For a Teddy Bear Hamster, tubes are generally not recommended. You can have one made especially for your hamster. However, the ones available commercially are never good enough for these hamsters.

  Keep adding and removing toys regularly to keep your hamster mentally stimulated. You must always ensure that you are not putting too much into the cage, as it will make the space crammed and uncomfortable.

It is necessary to get the cage ready before you bring the hamster home. That way you can lead him to his new enclosure and allow him to settle in. Making him change spaces too often can be uncomfortable, especially in case of Teddy Bear Hamsters that are too territorial.

Chapter 3: When the hamster is home

When you do bring the hamster home, there are several things that you need to consider. The first few days are crucial in making your hamster feel comfortable in your home. If you plan to play and cuddle with your hamster on day 1, it may not be a pleasant experience for you either.

1. Getting the hamster to settle in

The transition from a pet store, breeder or rescue shelter to your home is harder for your hamster than you imagine. Here are a few steps that will help make that transition a lot easier:

- Place your hamster in a fully prepped cage to ensure that there is no need to shift him around too much.

- When you buy bedding, food and substrate, try to keep it similar to the kind that he is already to used to. Only if the former material is not appropriate for a hamster should you change it. For example, if the hamster has been raised with cedar shavings as the substrate, make sure you change it.

- Place a light cloth over the cage. This will give the hamster some privacy and will prevent any distractions. That will allow him to explore the new space easily.

- Follow the four day rule. This means that your hamster should be left alone for four days before you actually interact with the hamster. The only interaction should be when you change the food and water. Many pet stores will even ask you to avoid eye contact entirely. While that is somewhat exaggerated, you will have to avoid too much closeness and interaction with him.

- Make sure that you do not allow any visitor or even members from your family to handle the hamster.

- They are very sensitive to loud noises. That means you have to keep him away from the television, stereo, etc. While the hamster will get used to the hustle and bustle in your home, it is never advisable to keep him in areas of the house that are too loud.

Even after the four day "curfew" be very gentle in your approach towards the hamster. You do not want to get too close too fast. You will have to tame your hamster first before you are comfortable enough to pick him up and play with him. We will talk about taming the hamster in the following sections.

2. Introducing your Teddy Bear Hamster to other pets

If you are bringing a hamster into a home that has an existing pet, it can be quite a hassle. You need to take a lot of special considerations when it comes to introducing your hamster to another pet. Remember that hamsters are really small and do not really have any natural defense. So, it makes them an easy target for pets like dogs and cats.

There are a lot of odd stories of cats and hamsters or dogs and hamsters getting along. This is quite a one off thing and you must always understand that they share the relationship of a predator and prey. In the real world, your cat or dog can cause some really serious damage to your hamster or can even kill him. If you notice any aggression, you may even have to place your hamster in an entirely different room.

You also need to remember that diseases can be transmitted from one animal to another. Although it is not very common for your hamster to get a disease from the dog and cat or vice versa, it can happen.

Your pet should not be allowed to scare the hamster. This means putting the cage in a place where the dog or cat can disturb it is not a good idea. They should not be able to bark at the cage or nudge it with their paws. If the pet licks or scratches the aquarium or cage, do not expect the hamster to appreciate it.

For hamsters, one of the biggest causes for all life threatening diseases is being stressed. Even conditions as severe as wet tail are a result of stress. So, keep an eye on your pet.

Your cat or dog should never be allowed to sit on the cage or sleep even when the hamster is away. This will lead to a lot of stress even if the hamster can smell the dog or cat. For all practical purposes, keeping the hamster cage away from your dog or cat is the best idea.

You have to ensure that the cat or dog cannot jump up or over the cage. If they knock it over, it will be fatal for the hamster.

You will also have to make sure that your cat or dog does not brush against the sides of the cage, especially if it is wired. Hamsters have the habit of pulling against the fur of the animal, making the latter very angry.

If you see that your cat or dog has begun to ignore the presence of the hamster, you can try to keep the cage in the same room. Then, when they are comfortable with the cage, you can bring the hamster out for a few minutes. But leaving them unattended together can be a bad idea. You can never say when the instinct will just kick in!

3. Children and Teddy Bear Hamsters

The Teddy Bear Hamster is one of the most recommended hamsters for children, mainly because the size makes them a lot easier to handle. But if your child is under 10 years of age, you do not want to expect them to handle a hamster independently. It is primarily because the child is not mature enough to handle a hamster on his own.

Children should be taught to approach a hamster cage with some amount of caution. Kids simply love these cute and cuddly creatures and will want to play with them right away. But, that can be hazardous.

You see, hamsters have poor vision and compromised depth perception. So when they are approached suddenly, they will become defensive. In the process, the child could get bitten or may harm the hamster by dropping him as a reflex. You should teach a child that a hamster should be approached slowly. Even if the child wants to reach in and just pet the furry creature, he/she will do so without startling him. Picking up and petting a Teddy Bear Hamster is not difficult as long as he is tame and as long as the child knows what has to be done.

With a Teddy Bear Hamster, you should also remember that the hamster probably will wake up after the child has fallen asleep. Then, when the child is awake, he will probably be asleep. So, unless your child is old enough to stay up to about 9 pm and spend some time with the hamster, he/she cannot handle the responsibility all alone.

Hamsters are a great option for a pet if you want to teach your child about the responsibility of having a pet. However, you need to make sure that you are available to assist the child when needed.

If your child is naughty, teases the hamster or knocks on the sides of the cage to scare the hamster, it is the worst thing for the health of the hamster. It will leave him extremely stressed and can cause some serious health issues.

In addition to that, you never know how the hamster will react to the child being playful. Unless you are sure about your child being able to handle him, it is best that you get him/her used to one by visiting friends who have a hamster or even taking him/her to pet stores or rescue shelters to meet one.

4. Tips to keep your hamster safe

A hamster is an extremely vulnerable creature because of its size. There have been several instances of a hamster getting trampled on or even getting stuck in door hinges. It is your job to make sure that your hamster is always safe in your home. Here are a few tips that will ensure that you do not have to worry about the hamster getting injured or meeting an untimely end.

- Keep the hamster in a space in your home that is quiet and not so bright. That will ensure that he does not get disturbed or startled by sudden sounds and movements.

- The hamster should not be exposed to sudden or drastic temperature changes. If it does get too cold, there are chances that your hamster will go into a state of hibernation. This will lead to a slowing down of breathing and reduced activity. While most owners think that their pet is dying, it is an indication that the temperature may be too low. In addition to that, if the room gets too warm, too soon, they could even develop heatstroke.

- If there are any large animals in your house, your hamster should be kept away from them. As we mentioned before, a cat or dog can really harm your hamster or even kill him.

- The cage should never be kept very high up on the top shelves. In case your hamster should escape, he can be seriously injured by falling off a high platform.

- In the case of Teddy Bear Hamsters, remember that they are very solitary creatures. You should never keep them in pairs. You must also avoid keeping hamsters of the opposite gender in the same cage, as they will mate and conceive. Each litter can have as many as 9 puppies.

- To avoid any chances of escaping, the bars of a wired cage should be close. You should also remember that the hamster's head or limbs should not get stuck in between. They have been known to mutilate themselves in an attempt to get free.

- In case you have a cage that has an open top, placing a mesh is advisable. If you are certain that the cage is tall enough to avoid any escapes, make sure that you do not add any accessory that the hamster can use to climb out of the cage.

- Whenever you want to play with your hamster or handle him, make sure that you wash your hands thoroughly. With this you have reduced chances of infection. In addition to that, make sure any food smell is removed from your hands, reducing the chances of getting bitten by your pet.

- When you get the hamster out of the cage, be very careful when you put him back. You must close all the doors and secure all the clasps. If your hamster does escape, you will have a hard time finding him.

- Check all the toys on a regular basis. If any of the toys have been broken or chewed on, they may have sharp edges that will lead to serious cuts and injuries. Whenever you clean the cage, make sure that you check the toys.

- If your hamster is not comfortable being handled, never pick him up and keep him at a height. Always handle him a few inches from the ground. A hamster that is nervous will jump! This can lead to some serious injuries. In most cases, they may even succumb to injuries to the head or the neck area.

- Grabbing a hamster suddenly or catching him off guard is not at all recommended. He will jump or might bite you really hard.

- A hamster should never be let out of the cage without supervision. There are dangers like being stepped on or even getting attacked by another pet in your home.

Besides all of this, you will also have to make sure that your home is hamster proof. That way it is safe for the hamster even if he does get away accidentally. Here are a few things that you should keep in mind:

- **All the power cords should be hidden:** Hamsters love to chew on wires. This puts them at the risk of being electrocuted or can start a fire in your home. Make sure that all the wires are secured in panels or are at least taped in a place where they will not be easy for the hamster to reach up to.

- **Any crack or hole in the wall must be filled:** You will have to make sure that the entire space that is remotely within reach of the hamster is taken care of. That way, you can be sure that there is nothing for the hamster to chew on. The more they chew, the larger the gaps will get. After a while, the hamster will be able to hide or actually escape through these holes.

- **Watch the plants around your home:** Some plants are poisonous for hamsters. You have to be extremely careful with plants like Amaryllis or lilies that can sprout a bulb. These plants are toxic for these creatures. If you are unsure of a plant being safe for hamsters, you should at least move it to another room for safety.

- **Look for smaller hazards:** If you see any loose nails lying about or any other sharp objects around the room, you must make sure that it is out of the way. Things that your hamster can knock down should be put out of the way. You must also be aware of loose threads or fibers that can get the legs of the hamster entangled.

If you do notice that your hamster is out of the cage, watch where you are stepping and be very careful about routine activities like vacuuming as they can lead to accidents with your pet. We will learn more about how you can look for a hamster that has escaped in the following section.

5. Looking for a lost hamster

Hamsters have always been known for being excellent escape artists. Your Teddy Bear Hamster is extremely intelligent and will find ways to get out of the cage if you are not cautious enough.

Just when you are about to get to bed, you may notice that your hamster is no longer in the cage. These nocturnal creatures escape mostly at night. You will have to make it a point to look for them immediately.

How often or how easily your hamster escapes depends entirely upon the personality of your pet. Some Teddy Bear Hamsters are so smart that they will actually learn to unlock the door of the cage. Others will like to gnaw their way through. In most cases, however, it is the fault of the owner for letting the door stay open. If you compromise on the quality of the cage, remember that your hamster will take very little time to actually chew his way through and get out if he actually plans to.

Now, if your hamster does escape, panic is not the answer. If you are lucky, you will find the hamster as soon as you notice that he has escaped. They will linger around often and will take some time to actually get "lost". If you look around and see that he is gone, it is time to start your search for your pet.

a. Where to look for a hamster

There are some spaces where your hamster is most likely to hide after escaping. For the most part, they like to just curl up in a small space that is warm. Hiding under things is also quite common with hamsters.

Here are some of the most common places that your hamster is likely to hide:

- Shoes: In case you have left your shoes out, a hamster will love to crawl into it. Teddy Bear Hamsters are likely to hide only in large shoes because of their size.

- Closets: If you leave a closet door even slightly open, your hamster is likely to rummage through your belongings. Using a flashlight is necessary of you have a large closet that the little fellow can get easily lost in.

- They are usually under the stove, a cupboard in the kitchen or under the fridge. This is the first place you want to look in as it can be most dangerous for your hamster.

- You can always look under furniture as hamsters love to hide under them. There will be several places for the hamster to hide in such as beneath the bed, dresser, futons, etc. There are also chances that your hamster will learn to make his way into a pillowcase or cushion case.

- Any shoebox or empty box is a place for a hamster to hide in. If there are any small boxes, you will notice that the hamster will love getting into it.

- There is always a good chance that your hamster is hiding under blankets. These blankets are extremely warm and cozy for the hamster.

- Hamsters simply love the bathroom. If you have soaps and shampoos that smell really nice, especially, your hamster will make frequent visits to the bathroom. The danger of drowning is always present. That is why you need to make sure that there is no way the hamster can get into the bathroom either through the door or through any gap under the door.

- If you have a radiator or heater in your house, your hamster is most probably in there. This is true only if the heater or radiator is not too hot. If it is warm, they will try to get in.

- Another common place for the hamster to escape into is the basement. It can be dark and scary for you to get in there but your hamster will simply love to be there. So, as a last resort, always look inside the basement.

There will be some spots that your hamster will pick as his favorite hiding spot. Make it a point to look there first when you notice that your hamster has pulled off another great escape.

b. How to track your hamster
If you are unable to find your hamster in any of the spots mentioned above, it is an uphill battle to locate him. However, you can use some of these tips to make this quest a lot easier on yourself with improved chances of finding the hamster:

- Always keep an eye at night. Even if this means staying up for a while, do it. Since all hamsters are nocturnal, they are most likely to move around after you have fallen asleep and there is a big chance that you will just miss him.

- In every room of your home, place a pile of sunflower seeds that you have counted. Then, if you notice that the number of seeds have reduced in any room, you have enough reason to believe that your hamster is in that room. However, this is not a guaranteed test, as the culprit could even be a mouse.

- It is also a good idea to sprinkle some cornstarch or flour around these seeds. If your hamster does steal the seeds, you will find a trail of footprints that will take you to the hiding place of the hamster.

- If you suspect any spot that the hamster could be hiding in, sprinkle some flour around it. Doorways are the best place to sprinkle flour in as the hamster is likely to cross at least one doorway when he is walking around.

- You will have to place some tinfoil or cellophane around the suspected areas. Then turn off all the lights. When the hamster walks over the foil or cellophane, you will be able to hear a noise that will help you locate him immediately.

- Take a yarn of wool and tie the strand to a peanut. If your hamster tries to gather the peanuts, you will see the trail of wool.

c. How to catch the hamster

If your hamster has been hand-tamed or is used to being handled, you will not find it as hard to catch him when he has escaped. However, if this was the hamster's first day or week in your home, here are a few tips that are sure to help you find and trap your hamster:

- Leave the cage door open and place some fresh food on the cage. In this case, there are chances that the hamster will just walk back in on his own. It will help to keep the cage around the areas that you suspect that he is hiding in. They will most probably eat the snack and take a nap. However, if you can stay up and close the door behind the hamster, you will keep him secure.

- A bucket trap is a great idea. Take a deep bucket that is enough to hold the hamster in but not so deep that he will hurt himself. Then, place a towel on the base of the bucket with some treats. Build a ramp using wood, leading to the bucket. Then, hope that the hamster will smell the treat and climb up the ramp and will jump in to get the treat. If the bucket is tall enough, he won't climb out of it. So make sure you pick a treat that is too good for the hamster to resist.

- You can even get a humane rat trap or a wired trap. This will catch the hamster without causing him any harm. Place a bait of peanut butter in the trap and wait for him to walk in. This should be your last resort, as the slightest accident can hurt the hamster quite severely.

6. Cleaning the hamster cage

You have to make sure that the cage that your hamster is living in is properly maintained. Hamsters are considered obsessive and compulsive by nature and will not tolerate any mess inside the cage. You will have to keep the cage clean with a regular routine if you want your hamster to be happy.

a. Daily cleaning

On a daily basis, it is a must to clean the food and water bowls. If the hamster has hoarded any food, take it out as it could harbor dangerous bacteria.

Remove any substrate that is soiled or wet and replace it with a clean one. If the bedding is soiled, it needs to be replaced too. For all the daily cleaning activities, wait until your hamster is active. That means you will have to do it in the evening. If you plan to do it while the hamster is sleeping you need to make sure that you do not wake him. He can get aggressive when woken and can even become extremely stressed.

b.Weekly cleaning
Every week, you have to clean the cage thoroughly. Here are six steps that will help you maintain a clean hamster cage without any hassle:

- Get the hamster out of the way. You will have to place him in another container or temporary carrier cage when you are cleaning up. That way you will not even have to worry about the hamster escaping while you are getting the cage cleaned out.

- Remove all the accessories, tunnels and toys from the cage. Wash them in soapy water and rinse with lukewarm water. Make sure that they are all dried fully before you place it back in. You can even leave them out in the sun to make sure that they are fully dry. You will have to get all the soap out, as any ingestion of the chemicals can make your hamster really sick.

- The bedding and the substrate should be removed completely. If you have a messy substrate like wood shavings, just place a garbage bag on one end of the cage and tip the contents into it. The cage should be fully empty. If your cage is free from any traces of soiled substrate, it will remain much cleaner for longer.

- You can purchase a disinfectant that is recommended for hamsters from a local pet store. These disinfectants do not contain any chemicals that may be hazardous to your pet. They do not even have any strong odor that will make the cage feel unfamiliar to the hamster. That way, you can be sure that the cage is fully clean without any compromises on the scent of the cage. You should just leave the disinfectant on for the recommended amount of time to ensure that it is fully dry before you add the new substrate or bedding. If you want to make the disinfectant at home, you have the option of mixing a cup of vinegar with a cup of water instead of buying one from a store.

- Place fresh bedding material and the substrate into the cage. You should make sure that the substrate is covering the floor of the cage fully. It should be thick enough to absorb the moisture as well.

- The bedding should also be fresh and your hamster should have enough to stay comfortably inside the cage. Do not move the placement of the bedding area, as the hamster has assigned specific spots for specific activities.

- All the toys and accessories should be placed back. You must ensure that they have all been placed exactly where they were before. Hamsters do not like their space being tampered with. They will remember where the accessories were placed and will not appreciate too many changes.

You can then place the hamster back in the cage with a bowl full of water and some fresh food to eat. Making sure that your hamster has a neat and clean environment is the mark of a responsible owner. That will also make sure that they are healthy and happy for a longer time. Remember the daily routine as well and do it at a specific time each day to make your hamster feel comfortable.

Chapter 4: Caring for your hamster

1. What to feed a hamster

It is important to ensure that your hamster gets clean and fresh food everyday. When you are feeding a hamster, remember that you are dealing with an animal who loves to eat. So, to avoid obesity and related issues, giving him good quality food is a must.

a. When to feed a hamster

The timing of the feed is very crucial. However, the dilemma is whether to feed the hamster in the morning or evening. Logically, it would seem ideal to feed him during the evening when he is actually awake.

However, there is research to support the fact that hamsters will wake up every two hours to grab a quick bite to eat. In that case, feeding in the morning is a good idea.

Let us look at the instinctive behavior of a hamster in the wild. Since they are nocturnal, they will gather all the treats at night and bring it back to the burrow. This stash of food will be consumed throughout the day.

The next question is how much you should feed a hamster. With the Teddy Bear Hamster, all you need to provide is a tablespoon of good food and then a good supplement of fresh produce. This is an approximation. The rule with hamsters is to give them all they can eat. You can even leave a variety of foods around the cage for them to enjoy all day long.

The amount of food that you are giving really depends upon the size of the food bowl. The hamster will choose how much to eat and when to eat. They have a good instinct for the grains that they want to eat as per the requirement of the body at a given time.

To aid growth and development, giving your hamster some protein is an absolute must. For this, you can give your hamster some dog biscuits or dry cat food. Biscuits are a better choice for your hamster as it will also aid in grinding the teeth of the hamster down as he gnaws at the biscuit.

b. Are treats necessary?

Having a few treats available can work wonders in helping your hamster calm down when you are handling them. There are a few foods that you can give your hamster as a treat which will also double as a nutritional supplement. This is a list of foods approved by most vets and pet dieticians:

- Eggs: there is no better source for protein than eggs. The good news is that hamsters simply love eggs. If you have a pregnant hamster at home, it is especially beneficial. However, you must give eggs occasionally to your hamster. You will also make sure that it is cleaned from the cage within 24 hours. That way you will not have any rotting food in the cage.

- Fish liver oil: you can soak a grain in fish liver oil and give it to your hamster. He will absolutely love it. He also gets vitamins A and D through this. Another option is to buy puppy food that is fortified with fish liver oil.

- Meat: Whether you can give your hamster meat or not is a matter of great debate. Now, for some it is an encouragement for habits like cannibalism. However, with research conducted on hamsters bred by breeders, cannibalism has not been reported upon providing meet. Small chunks of mutton or meal worms can be provided. You must never give a hamster pork.

- Milk: This makes a great treat. But, giving it in a bowl increases the chances of it being tipped over. In addition to that, milk may also turn sour if the day is warm. You can give milk rarely but avoid giving it to ill stock, young hamsters and pregnant hamsters. You must also ensure that the dish is fully cleaned before the milk turns sour.

- Mixed bird seed: The seeds meant for budgerigars and canaries are the best option and are highly nutritious for hamsters. You can mix it with the grains you give your hamster.

- Monkey chow: This is a type of kibble that makes for a great hamster treat. This supplement is wonderful, as it contains nutritious ingredients such as wheat germ, corn, brewer's yeast, proteins and whole eggs. You must not provide this more than once a week. This is also a wonderful treat to give your hamster as it helps grind the teeth completely and keep it short.

- Yeast: This is a great source of Vitamin B that is necessary for the nervous system of your hamster. Hamsters are usually very anxious and it is possible to reduce stress exceptionally with this supplement. Since stress is one of the primary causes of diseases like wet tail, giving your hamster an occasional pinch of this treat is a great idea. You can get nutritional yeast from any health store. It is not bitter and will actually be enjoyed quite thoroughly by your hamster.

Alternatively, you can also give your hamster half a yeast tablet that you can get quite easily in most pet stores. When you give your hamster these tablets, make sure you use the ones that have no flavor. Garlic flavored yeast can cause kidney issues in your hamster.

Treats must never replace food. It is very easy to do this with hamsters because of the small amount of food that they consume. It should only be used when you want to calm your hamster down. In addition, you must remember that no treat should be provided more than once a day.

c. Using food bowls
With hamsters, whether you should use a food bowl or not is an often debated subject. Some experts believe that scattering the food on the floor of the cage is more beneficial. In the wild, hamsters are hoarders. So, they will collect food all day and actually stay stimulated.

On the other hand, when your hamster is given food in a bowl, he will not really feel the need to hoard as he sees the food in one place. The only time you will see the hamster displace food from the bowl is when you have a pregnant hamster that wants to feed her babies. That is when the food will be taken from the bowl to the nest.

There are some advantages of using a bowl, however. You can closely monitor the amount of food that your hamster has eaten. If the grains are on the floor, on the other hand, there is no way of telling. You can make sure that your hamster gets clean food each day by cleaning out all the leftovers from it.

d. Balancing the diet
There are some nutrients that are a must have for hamsters. You will have to ensure that all of these are available for the hamster to be in great health. In fact, some foods are dependent on the others for the proper utilization of the nutrients.

There are some primary items that you need in a balanced diet:

- Carbohydrates and fats: These nutrients are needed to keep the body of the hamster warm. Of course, you should not provide this excessively, as it will be stored in the body as fat. That will cause serious issues with breeding and will lead to poor health. You can provide foods like yeast, sugar, potato, barley, oats, corn and wheat as good sources of these nutrients.

- Proteins: Proteins, just like in humans, are needed to build the tissues and to help the hamster grow. They are especially important for pregnant hamsters and young hamsters. Some of the best sources of protein are beans, barley, corn, nuts, peas and wheat.

- Vitamins: Hamsters need a small amount of vitamins. However, if they do not get the amount needed, the health repercussions are quite extreme. Fresh produce is the best source of vitamins for hamsters.

- Minerals: You will need vitamins also in small amounts. The best sources are green foods, vegetables, milk and grains.

- Water: Water is needed for the hamster to be able to absorb all the nutrients mentioned above. But, make sure you provide this with a bottle instead of a water dish, as the dish will be tipped over very easily.

Providing your hamster with a balanced meal is crucial for his health. Even though they have been domesticated, hamsters will eat just about anything that is before them. They continue to have the same pattern of metabolism, instincts, lifestyles and nutritional requirements as their ancestors. Essentially, hamsters hail from the drier parts of the world. That means that their foods will consists of insects, wild grass, grains that they can get from farms nearby and vegetables.

A balanced diet can be provided for your hamster with foods like corn, oats, sunflower seeds, rabbit pellets, alfalfa pellets, wheat, barley, dehydrated vegetables, cat food and dog biscuits. Some of them are used as the main feed and the others can be provided as supplementary treats from time to time.

You will be able to find commercially made hamster mixes that are prepackaged. This is found in most pet stores and will consist of all the basic nutrients required by a hamster. Providing fresh fruits and vegetables about thrice a week can do wonders for your pet hamster.

When you include a variety of foods in the diet of your hamster, he will choose whatever he needs for his good health. You can even maintain a record of the foods that he eats and the foods that he rejects to understand what his favorite grains are.

You must never give your hamster chocolate or refined sugar treats. This will not provide any value to the diet of the hamster. It will also get stuck in the pouch of the hamster, creating damage that cannot be treated. It is best that you avoid any commercially-prepared treats for hamsters, as they will consist of a lot of sugar.

The diet of your hamster is one of the most important aspects of pet care. You may feel like spoiling your hamster from time to time. But this can be very unhealthy for your hamster. It is best that you pick only foods that are approved for hamsters and proven to be beneficial.

e. Approved foods for hamsters

Some foods are good and others can be disastrous for your hamster's health. For instance, a diet heavy in sugars can lead to diabetes in your hamster. So you need to know what foods are safe. The rule is that any fresh produce that you give your hamster should be rinsed well and dried before giving it to the hamster. You must also make sure that the food does not contain any pesticides.

Here is a list of foods that you can give your hamster:

Fruits:
- Banana
- Apple
- Blueberries
- Blackberries
- Cherries
- Cantaloupe
- Lychee
- Grapes
- Melon
- Mango
- Plums
- Peaches
- Raspberry leaves
- Raspberry
- Strawberries

You must make sure that the fruits you give the hamster should not contain the pit or the stone. They contain toxins that will be harmful of your pet.

Vegetables:
- Bean sprouts
- Asparagus
- Broccoli

- Bok Choy
- Carrots
- Cabbage
- Celery
- Cauliflower
- Chard
- Chickweed
- Chestnuts
- Clover
- Chicory
- Cucumbers
- Corn
- Endive
- Dandelion leaves
- Kale
- Green Beans
- Peas
- Parsnips
- Radicchio
- Spinach
- Roman lettuce
- Squash
- Sweet bell peppers
- Sweet potatoes
- Turnip
- Swiss Chard
- Water cress
- Water chestnut
- Zucchini

Meats or protein sources:
- Cooked ground beef without any grease
- Low fat cottage cheese
- Cooked turkey or chicken
- Mealworms
- Grasshoppers from pet stores
- Crickets from pet stores
- Tofu
- Eggs
- Whole grain bread
- Low fat yoghurt

- Monkey chow
- Lab blocks
- Plain dog biscuits

Others:
- Baby food
- Cheese
- Buckwheat
- Cooked pasta
- Cooked brown rice
- Flax seed
- Dry toast Pumpkin seeds
- Sugarless cereal
- All nuts except almonds
- Lentils
- Squash seeds
- Nutritional yeast
- Wheat germ and bran
- Alfalfa
- Peanuts
- Plain pop corn

Foods that you must AVOID:
- Chocolate
- Almonds
- Canned foods
- Apple seeds
- Pork and its products
- Candies
- Raw potato
- Eggplant
- Raw kidney beans
- Avocado
- Grape seeds
- Fool's parsley
- Tomato leaves
- Rhubarb leaves
- Tangerines
- Oranges
- Watermelon
- Peach leaves and stones

- Cherry stone
- Apricot stone
- Lime
- Lemons
- Spices
- Jams
- Jellies
- Onion
- Garlic
- Leeks
- Pickles
- Chives
- Scallions

Choose from the foods that are approved for a hamster by health experts and you can be sure that you will have a healthy and happy pet throughout. It also ensures that you will have good litters if you plan to breed your hamster.

When it comes to hamster care, food plays a vital role because hamsters love to eat. They will need to nibble for various reasons besides nutrition such as keeping the teeth ground and even to prevent any chances of boredom.

2. How to handle a hamster

By nature, hamsters are afraid of almost everything that is not a hamster, so you should learn how to handle one well.

First, unless you notice that your hamster requires some medical attention or could be in pain, you will never wake a sleeping hamster. They get very stressed and will become defensive if you wake them up from deep slumber. You will most probably end up with a big bite on your finger or arm. Hamster bites are really nasty and can be very deep and painful.

Hamsters also have very poor eyesight. That means that they rely on just one sense, which is the sense of smell. The second most important hamster sense is sound. So, before you approach your hamster, allowing him to use these senses to know who you are will make him comfortable and will keep you relaxed as well.

If you are planning to pick up your hamster, make sure that your hands are thoroughly washed. You don't want him to believe that your hand is food because there is a hint of your last meal's smell on your hand. That may also make him want to take a good nibble of your arm.

When taming your hamster, you have to be extremely cautious. They are aggressive creatures, which means that you will need to be extremely patient. You will start working with your hamster every evening. You have to wait until your hamster is awake and active.

In the initial attempts, there is the danger of your hamster jumping out of your hands. You will have to make sure that you do not keep the cage at a height. Working around an open cage is the best option. Never reach in and stun the hamster. That is when he will show his aggressive side. The signs to watch out for are teeth showing, the hamster rolling on his back and his claws up. If he shows these signs, you will not even try to pick him up. Just let him calm down and relax.

Once he is relaxed, you will give him a treat and just touch his back gently. That shows that him that touching is a good thing. The hamster may get comfortable instantly or may take a while before he is confident with being picked up by you. Keep trying until the hamster is relaxed when he sees your hand approaching.

When your hamster is ready, you will scoop him up gently. Do not attempt to grab him as you can hurt him. Now, there may be a chance of squealing when you do this. Usually, a hamster that squeals will not bite. However, there are a few exceptions and you have to be cautious. Pick him up gently when he stops squealing. That is a sign that he is no longer worried about being touched by you.

The first time you pick your hamster up, stay low and hold him close to you. Jumping is a common problem with hamsters and since they do not have very good depth perception, they do not understand how high they really are if you are standing up. That is when they end up having serious injuries and wounds because you cannot control how they land on the floor.

You can keep the hamster calm while he is in your hands. Stroking the back is a very good idea. At the same time, you can also gently stroke the forehead. Some prefer being touched on the forehead. Keep these interactions short. If you see that the hamster is getting restless, just let him into the cage and give him a treat. Keep doing this with increased time periods until the hamster knows that being touched and handled is not all bad. If you already have a hand tamed hamster that you got from a breeder or a pet store, it should be much easier to handle him.

Here are some dos and don'ts to sum up the process of handling and taming your hamster.

Dos:

- Keep talking to him in a gentle voice
- Keep your movements towards him very slow when trying to pick him up
- Wash your hands well every time you pick him up so that he gets one scent each time you approach him
- Let him smell you first to understand what is approaching him
- Let the hamster calm down. Never attempt a pick up especially if he seems defensive to you.

Don'ts:
- Never make any jerky or big movements as it will scare your hamster who is quite defensive at this point
- Do not make loud noises when you are approaching him as you will startle him
- Do not hold him high up, as he has every chance of falling
- Never ever pick up a hamster that is sleeping.

You will have to use these tips for everyone in your family who wants to handle the hamster. At no point should you assume that a hamster that is comfortable being handled by you will be comfortable with everyone. Yes, a tame hamster is easier to approach and befriend but nothing should happen suddenly.

3. Bathing your hamster
Normally, hamsters will keep themselves clean and will not require frequent baths. But there may be instances when there is something like paint or varnish on the coat. In addition to that, basic hygiene is required to make sure that your hamster does not get any diseases that are related to bacterial or fungal deposits, which can come from mud deposits or dirt on the fur. This is the only time when you will clean your hamster. If not, you put him at the risk of catching a chill because the essential and natural oils have been removed from his body. You can use a substrate like Chinchilla sand that your hamster can use to clean himself regularly.

Now, if there is a situation when you need to give your hamster a bath, here are a few steps that you may follow:

- Pour some lukewarm water in a bowl. The depth should not be greater than 2 inches. Elbow testing the water will tell you whether it is the right temperature or not. Just dip your elbow in the bowl and you will know.

- Place the hamster in the bowl and wet him gently. The area that is dirty can be rubbed gently to clean it. Now, you have to be very careful to prevent the chances of water getting into the nose, ears, mouth and eyes. A hamster inhaling liquid is a disaster. It can even prove to be fatal.

- If the coat has something that is extremely sticky and difficult to remove, you can use baby shampoo. This again should not be used on the face. If the face is dirty, you will only use water and rub the area clean.

- The shampoo must be thoroughly rinsed to prevent any consumption of the chemicals in the shampoo.

- Place the hamster on a towel and dry him thoroughly. Be very careful about the legs getting caught in the fabric.

- You may use a hairdryer that is low in power. On the lowest setting, it is safe to dry your hamster. Keep the hairdryer away from the body of the hamster and keep your hand in between to ensure that you do not get too much heat on his body. The hairdryer can burn the skin if you are not careful.

- When you are washing your hamster, it is advisable to choose a day that is warmer to prevent any chances of the hamster catching a chill.

- Before you put the hamster back into the cage, he should be fully dry. If not the bedding material may stick to the fur of your hamster, making him dirty again.

Word of caution: The method mentioned above is not safe for a hamster. In fact, no method of cleaning him is safe. So avoid it entirely unless you think that he could be harmed by the substance on his skin or fur. This is a risky method but is definitely the best of other options like using a hand shower etc. If you are unsure about cleaning your hamster properly, it is best to take him to a vet who will help you.

A smelly hamster is not always a dirty hamster. He could be ready to breed or may even have a condition that has affected his skin. When you feel like your hamster is smelly, taking him to a vet is the best option available to you.

One way to keep the hamster hygienic is to ensure that his surroundings are clean and safe. Remove all toxic substances that can cling on to his fur and cause health issues. Regular cleaning of the cage is the best thing you can do for your hamster's health and well-being.

5. Grooming your hamster

While bathing your hamster is not really important, you have to groom your hamster well for his safety as well as your own. There are some routine practices that will ensure that your hamster is always well groomed.

a. Nail trimming

Usually, hamsters will maintain their nails by burrowing and digging. However, as they get older, these habits reduce and will lead to the nails becoming overgrown. This can also happen if there isn't enough bedding material for him to dig into.

Even an obese hamster will have nail overgrowth. Basically, being active will help your hamster keep his nails short. If the hamster stops important activities like climbing, running and digging, you will have to deal with overgrown nails. Then, trimming the nails becomes important to make sure that you do not get scratched when you pick the hamster up. Additionally, overgrown nails tend to get caught in things inside the cage, leading to injuries.

Hamster nails curl inwards. When neglected for too long, they will dig into the skin on the hamster's feet. This will also get infected with time.

With nail trimming, you have two options:

• First, you can give the hamster options to keep the nails short himself. That means you can place sandpaper with fine grits in one corner of the cage. Do not cover the floor of the cage with this, as it will irritate his paw and make it sore. Using sandpaper on a ramp or in the wheel is good idea. You can even place the sandpaper in a maze or a tube meant for your hamster. This way, every time your hamster walks in a certain area or uses these accessories, the friction will lead to the nails getting trimmed automatically.

• Second, you can use a nail clipper. This is the harder option but with a little patience you should be able to learn to do this properly. The only challenge is to get the hamster to stay put while you clip his nails to ensure that you do not cut off the quick. The quick is that part of the nail that contains the nerves and the blood in the nail. If you cut this accidentally, you can cause a lot of bleeding and put the hamster in pain. Using a small clipper that is used for kittens is a good idea, as you can gently cut the area just above the quick. The nails of the hamster are light in color. That enables you to see the quick. If you can see it, you can easily clip the nails without worrying about hurting the hamster. If you are unsure, you may want to ask your vet to teach you how to do this properly at home. It will take some time and patience too clip each nail of your Teddy Bear Hamster. If not, you can have it done by professionals at costs as low as $10 or £5.

b. Tooth trimming

As long as your hamster has enough stuff to chew and food to nibble on, it is rare that they will need tooth trimming. They will keep their teeth healthy on their own. But if the hamster is unwell or has hurt a tooth, he will have the issue of overgrown teeth. You will know that your hamster has overgrown teeth when one tooth is longer than the other or if the tooth looks like it has an abnormal size. This leads to more painful bites and can even lead to the hamster hurting himself.

You can clip the teeth but remember that it is not easy to do. If you have never done this before, make sure you take your hamster to the vet and ask for assistance. They will be able to show you how to do it safely. In addition to that, it is advisable to have the teeth checked because there are chances of some underlying illness.

You also need to be sure that your hamster actually needs a tooth clipping. If it is not needed, you will be causing a lot more harm.

The principle of tooth clipping is that you need a steady and confident hand that will also keep your hamster comfortable. Once you are sure of that, here are some steps that you can follow:

- Hold the hamster in a towel. That will give you better grip on your hamster.

- When you are clipping the hamster's teeth, you will need two people. If you have assistance, it is safer. One person will hold the hamster and get a grip on him with the scruff of the neck. That will make the pet immobile and will make him open the mouth. You can never force a hamster's mouth open.

- Again, you may use a cat nail clipper for this. The cut that you make should be towards the mouth. The slant should be inwards.

- Keep an eye on the tongue and the cheek of your hamster. It should not get in the middle of the teeth and the clippers. If your hamster is moving around, it will spell disaster.

- Every tooth should be cut individually. If you do them together, chances are that they will shatter or split.

- Once you have cut the teeth, you can file it using a nail file to make them safe.

If you feel, at any point, that you are unable to safely trim the teeth, do not attempt to do it, as it may cause unnecessary injuries to the animal.

c. Combing

Teddy Bear Hamsters are longhaired. Therefore, you need to keep their fur well groomed. That means your hamster will have to be brushed on a regular basis. In some cases, trimming the fur slightly is also useful.

Brushing the fur of your Teddy Bear Hamster has several benefits. You will see that food particles, pieces of the bedding and other material are usually lodged in the long fur. It can be a challenge for the hamster to get it all out while they groom themselves. Matting is also an issue with these hamsters, although it is quite rare.

The best way to brush your Teddy Bear Hamster is using a hairbrush. Pick your hamster out of the cage, give him a treat to relax him and then brush his fur. Keep talking to your hamster as you brush his hair. Once he is comfortable and engaged, it will become easier on you.

Just place the tooth brush near the neck of the hamster and move it slowly. Rub it back and forth to remove any debris. If there is any matting, it can be removed using a fine comb. Once the fur is clean, you can brush in the direction of the fur to make it smooth.

Having a well-groomed hamster also reduces the chances of any health issues and makes your hamster look really cute. With Teddy Bear Hamsters, particularly, grooming may be required from time to time, although not very regularly.

6. Finding a good vet

When you are looking for a good vet for your hamster, you will need to find someone who specializes in small animal treatment. While a regular vet should be able to help you for the most part, finding a small animal facility will ensure that the equipment available will be beneficial to your hamster when there is an emergency.

A vet who specializes in hamsters should, preferably, be a part of the Association of Exotic Mammal Veterinarians. This will guarantee that he/she has the skills needed to treat a small animal, if not a hamster in particular.

If you are unable to locate a vet who is a part of this association, you can look up the website of the American Board of Veterinary Practices. This will give you a list of individuals who are available in the vicinity of your home.

It is good to follow up this research with a quick study of the testimonials provided locally. If you just see one positive review or one negative review, it means that there is something unusual about this. Online reviews are often rigged and therefore provide one source of quality check, albeit not a very dependable one.

You can then call the vets you have listed for your zone. Asking them three simple questions will be able to tell you a lot about the hamster practice of the facility you have called.

- How many hamsters do you treat in a week?
- I have an emergency with my hamster. Can you tell me what I can apply on the wound on his back?
- How much would it cost to spay a hamster?

You can assess the answers that they give you to see if they are confident and accurate about them. If there is any hesitation, it will tell you that the facility is not very well versed with hamster treatment.

In a hamster facility that deals mostly with hamsters, you will notice that they see a minimum of 10 hamsters a week. Now in a local vet facility, you will see that only about two hamsters are seen every month. That may lead to an unpleasant experience when your hamster has an emergency, mainly because they are not equipped.

When you ask about the wound of your hamster, if Neosporin is recommended, it is your first clue that you have to look for an alternative. Since this ointment contains bacitracin and neomycin that is life threatening to hamsters, causing serious diarrhea, it will not be recommended. Even a small amount of ingestion of these ingredients can be extremely harmful for your hamster.

Now, this question is good to ask as it will become a lead for a better hamster vet. If you ask a less experienced hamster vet about spaying, they will recommend you to someone else. On the other hand, if the facility that you call is comfortable dealing with the spaying surgery, they should be able to treat any other medical condition that your hamster may have.

Chapter 5: Understanding Hamster Hibernation

If you live in an area that gets too cold, you probably have ways of staying warm such as wearing a sweater or keeping your socks on. Now, even though the hamster has a nice furry coat, they are not able to handle the cold very well. Genetically, they have evolved in the warmer areas of the world.

Although they have been popularly kept as pets, hamsters have not evolved to enjoy the cold too much. If the temperature drops suddenly, it can have dangerous repercussions for them because the body will slip into hibernation.

1. Understanding hibernation

At some point, hamsters will reduce their usual physical activity and will reduce their metabolism quite drastically. We normally associate the idea of hibernation with bears. They tend to eat a lot just before the hibernation season and store a lot of fat to support them during this stage. Since the heart rate is low, breathing is low, metabolism reduces and the body slows down overall, they do not really need as much energy.

The concern with all Syrian hamsters including the Teddy Bear Hamster is that they are not the best at hibernating. The only threat to them is dehydration during this stage.

Hibernation is the last survival option for hamsters and is not really ideal. While they are able to slow down all bodily processes and are even able to store fat, they are unable to retain water.

2. Preventing hamster hibernation

The most common reason for hibernation is when the temperature drops very drastically. However, there are chances that your hamster will also begin to hibernate if there is a slight fluctuation of temperature combined with a lack of water and food. So, there are chances that, if your hamster is not given enough food, he will slip into hibernation even during the warmer months.

Here are some steps that you can take to prevent hamster hibernation:

• Check on your hamster every morning and evening to see if he is active.

- In case there are any drafts in your hamster's area, keep him away from it.

- Make sure your hamster cage is housed in the warmer areas of your home.

- During the colder months, you can try to elevate the temperature around the cage of the hamster. While electric heaters may be used, they do very little to maintain the temperature at a constant. They can heat up too much too soon. So, it is a better option to place a heating pad below your hamster's cage.

- A reptile heating pad that is meant to be placed under tanks is a good idea and is a better option in comparison to human heating pads. These pads are self-regulating and can be left on at all times.

- Place the pads in all four corners of the cage to raise it by about an inch. That way the hamster will be warm but will not get too hot.

- Some pet stores may recommend heated rocks, which are meant for reptiles. These stones are not even safe for reptiles. They can melt the cage and can lead to burns and bruises on the belly and feet.

- Even if your hamster is in a nesting phase and seems to have built a nest that looks extremely cosy, it does not mean that he is warm and will not go into hibernation. In fact, if the nest is too large, it is a clue that your hamster is trying very hard to keep himself warm in a room that is too cold.

3. Symptoms of hibernation
Here are some signs to watch out for if you think your hamster is hibernating. In most cases, people think that the hamster is actually dead.

- He will appear to be dead and motionless
- His breathing will be very weak
- The hamster is limp and not stiff as he would be in case of death
- The ears, nose and the feet and other areas with less fur will seem ice cold
- The body will be cold as well.

4. What to do when the hamster hibernates?
You need to follow these important measures to ensure that your hamster comes out of hibernation so that he can rehydrate himself.

- Let him get warm. Bring the hamster to a room that is warmer. If you can, place a few towels on a heating source and place the hamster on it. Use a heating bag preferably. Cover your hamster with a towel too. Make sure he is only partially covered.

- Next, you can rub your hamster. Do not do it too vigorously. This movement will warm the body up and will also help you wake your pet up.

- Keep a medicine dropper handy. Even a syringe should do. When your hamster does wake up, the first thing to do would be to provide him with some liquid. If he licks on the syringe and tries to swallow it, it is a great sign.

- As for the liquid, you can give him water mixed with Pedialite instead of just water. This is an energy-producing liquid with electrolytes that will help him recover from hibernation faster.

- If Pedialite is not available, you can even mix one teaspoon of sugar in a cup of water. The sugar will give him the boost of energy that he needs. Hamsters love sugar and it will work well to get your hamster to respond.

- As the hamster gets more energy, he will become perkier and will drink the liquid offered to him more actively. He will keep the eyes open a little.

- You will need to work to keep the hamster awake. This means that you need to give him some soft foods that are hamster safe to get his attention.

- The best options for a hamster waking up from hibernation are fat free chicken broth, mashed potatoes, baby foods, pureed vegetables and oatmeal. Any food that he can lick off your finger is a good idea.

- Keep offering the liquid. Prevent dribbles and wipe off any with tissue paper, as it will not help keep the hamster warm.

5. Other tips on hibernation
There are a few things that you can expect with a hamster that has just come out of hibernation. You need not worry about these issues too much, as you can nurse your hamster back to health with some consistent care and patience.

- The hamster will be entirely limp in the beginning. He will just lie on the belly with all the limbs stretched out.

- When he wakes up you will notice that he will increase movement slightly and will be able to gain control. The eyes will open up first and then the nose and whisker may twitch.

-

- He will be able to lift his head although he may not be able to hold it up for too long. It will take him some time to gain control over his head.

- As he begins to get into a state of wakefulness, he will pull his limbs from beneath and will hold a crouched body position.

- The hamster will try to take slow steps and may just wobble around the cage. Until he gets complete control over the body, he will shake a lot and may even shiver. This looks a little unsettling but is absolutely normal for your hamster.

- As the temperature of the body begins to get back to normal, there will be twitches and spasms in the muscles. This stage can take about one hour to get to. It may even take longer but as long as your hamster is making progress, you have nothing to worry about.

- Continue rubbing and feeding the hamster and he will improve quickly. Sometimes, it will take about three hours for him to get back to his normal self. Then, you will see him walk around like nothing happened at all.

If after all these attempts the hamster is not revived or does not show any signs of being better, and you are sure that he is still alive, it may be time to take him to the vet.

6. Hibernation aftercare

Once the hamster is back on his feet, here are some things that you need to keep in mind:

- Place the cage in a quiet and warm place.

- Make sure that he has a lot of water and food and let him recover on his own.

- Add half a Pedialite to the water for two or three days to give him more energy.

- The bedding should be fresh. You may even have to provide the hamster with some nesting material.

- Check on the hamster every 45 minutes the following day to make sure that he is comfortable.

If you have given him all the favorable conditions required, he should be up and going the next day. You may even see him running on the hamster wheel in a few days' time.

Chapter 6: Travelling with a Hamster

You may decide to go on a vacation with your hamster. Or you may be shifting homes and want to bring the hamster along. Either way, it would be important to understand the right way to travel with your hamster.

The trouble with hamsters is that they can get really stressed when you travel with them. So, it is your responsibility to ensure that your hamster is comfortable irrespective of the mode of travel that you are choosing for him.

1. Travelling by car

Car travel is relatively easier for hamsters. They are able to enjoy short rides, in fact. All you need to do is make sure that the conditions of travel are conducive for the hamster.

When you are travelling by car, here are a few things to keep in mind:

- Make sure you have ample bedding and treats if you are going to be travelling for a longer period of time.

- The cage should be cleaned a day in advance to get the hamster accustomed to the new bedding. It also prevents the chances of having to travel with a smelly cage in your car.

- You need to be careful about packing your hamster into the car. Now, if you do not have any seats vacant, the best place to put the hamster cage is on the floor of the rear seat. You can even get someone to hold it on their lap if the ride is not too long.

- Placing the cage on the luggage is never a good idea. When you hit the brakes, the cage may fling forward and stress the hamster out. You could also injure someone sitting in your car.

- Check on the hamster regularly to make sure he is okay. If he looks too cold or seems uncomfortable, control the air conditioning in your car. Maintaining it at room temperature is best for the hamster.

- There may also be the need for a little more food and water. If you find the water or food containers empty, it is time for a refill. Remember that sudden temperature changes are quite common while travelling. If the hamster, additionally, does not have water and food, he may even slip into hibernation.

- If you notice that your hamster is stressed or scared, never try to handle him unless you want a nasty bite on your hand. Instead, call him to you and offer him a treat. That will make him a lot more relaxed. Taking breaks while travelling is recommended if you are travelling with your hamster. That way you get to check up on him and you will also be able to calm him down.

- Staying at a motel or hotel requires some homework. You should be certain that the hamster is allowed in the hotel.

- You will never leave the hamster inside the car. With you away, the car is an area with new smells that will make him really stressed. In addition to that, you will also see that temperatures inside a car increase drastically. This can be fatal for your hamster.

Even though your hamster is a small animal, it is necessary to take him very seriously when you are travelling with him. Keeping him hydrated and ensuring that he is comfortable is entirely your responsibility. Now, when you are travelling with your hamster, it is a good idea to give him vegetables to keep him hydrated. If the water bottle leaks, he may not even get near it and may suffer from dehydration.

2. Travelling by plane

Unless it is absolutely necessary, it is ill advised to take your hamster on a plane. The conditions inside an aircraft can be too extreme for the body of the hamster to handle. So, if you can leave the hamster behind with a friend or relative who can simply feed him, it is the best option.

However, if you decide to move overseas or move to a different state, you might want to take your hamster along with you. That is quite a natural feeling. Yet, for the safety of the hamster, finding him a new home is the best option.

In any case, if you must travel with your hamster, here are a few steps to follow:

- Contact as many airlines as you can. Look for one that allows you to take small animals on board.

- It is even better if they will allow you to keep him in the cabin with you.

- Some of the airlines may expect you to place your hamster along with the other pets in the pet cargo. That is not an option to consider.

- In the plane cargo, there may be several unfamiliar sounds and noises that will only scare your hamster. In addition to that, a pet cargo can get really cold. This is disastrous for a hamster, as it will slip into hibernation or may even die.

- You must also consider the temperature fluctuations when you are travelling by plane. For instance, the tarmac is very hot while the aircraft itself is freezing cold. Hamsters never do well with extreme temperature changes.

- Travelling with your hamster at your feet in the cabin at least allows you to keep a close eye on your pet. You may have to fly cabin class in most airlines for facility.

- Having a carrier that is approved by the airlines is mandatory. Make sure you check about the requirements beforehand.

- Some airlines will ask for a health certificate for your hamster as well.

- You will have to follow several guidelines and even give them in writing that you will not hold them responsible if something were to happen to your hamster.

- All the info required should be kept easily available with your tickets. That way you can present it as soon as you check in.

In any case, with all the hassles involved with customs quarantine and also the risk that you will be putting your hamster at, it is better to leave the hamster home unless it is absolutely necessary to take him by plane.

3. Pet sitter for your hamster

If you have to go away without the hamster, it is necessary to look for someone who can clean the bedding, clean the cage and of course, give your hamster food and water.

It depends upon how long you are gone really. If it is just for a few days, you can even ask a neighbor to give your hamster some food in the morning and evening. A friend or relative can do this for you too.

Another option that you have is to leave your hamster at a friend or relative's place. That way, you are sure that there will be no missed schedule at least in your hamster's feeding and water requirements.

However, if these options are not available to you, you may need to opt for a pet sitter. It is an option to look for professionals but you may end up paying them exorbitantly for basic tasks like feeding as well.

But, having a professional helps when you are away for a long time. They will know how to take care of the hamster's requirements, including cleaning the cage safely.

The final option that you could consider is pet boarding. There are several facilities that are available in all major cities. The only thing you need to be sure of is that they also cater to small animals like hamsters.

Sometimes, your vet may have a pet boarding facility. This is a lot more trustworthy, as your hamster is also familiar with the environment.

If you are putting your hamster in a pet boarding facility, make sure you pay a visit to ensure that they have other small animals, too. A glance at their cages will give you an idea about the quality of the pet boarding. If the animals look clean and active, then it is a good place to leave your pet behind.

Chapter 7: Breeding Hamsters

Many hamster parents take to breeding them as a hobby. While breeding a hamster can be a lot of fun, it is also a big responsibility. Only when you know that you are sure about breeding a hamster should you consider this.

1. Ask yourself these questions

Before you even decide to breed your hamster, here is a list of questions that you must ask yourself:

- How do you know when a female hamster is in heat? And how often does she go into heat?

- Are there at least 20 people available to take the pups when you have these litters?

- In case you decide to keep them all yourself, are you able to house 20 cages in your home considering that you cannot keep two Teddy Bear Hamsters in one cage?

- If anything were to go amiss, would you be able to hand feed the offspring?

- Do you know how to figure out the bloodline of the parents and whether there are any genes that can harm the puppies?

- Do you have any idea about the gestation period?

- How will you introduce the territorial male to a hormonal female Teddy Bear Hamster?

- What are your reasons for breeding the hamsters?

- Do you know how many litters will be born in each season?

- What will you do once the male or the female is infertile? Will you still keep them?

- Will you be able to provide the diet that the mother needs during the pregnancy?

- Are you prepared for any possible disaster?

- Are you prepared for emotional trauma related to common hamster issues such as cannibalism or death of the puppies?

These questions will help you learn about breeding and whether you are really ready to become a hands-on hamster breeder who can provide a humane and conducive environment for the mother and the puppies.

2. Preparing to breed hamsters

The first thing that you want to do is understand why you want to breed the hamsters in the first place. Don't do it unless you have a good reason. You must breed your hamsters only if:

- You want to have more hamsters at home as pets
- You want to sell them
- You intend to give away hamsters to good homes

Understand how the hamsters will be advertised. You need to be aware of the fact that it is very hard to find good homes for the hamster puppies. You will need to place advertisements in papers or in local pet stores. Today, even social media plays a vital role in finding pets good homes. When you know that you will be able to find a good number of people to take these hamsters home, you can think about breeding them.

Once this has been clearly determined, the next step is to make sure that you have all the supplies required to provide a good environment for the hamsters to breed in.

You must always get unrelated hamsters to breed if you want a successful litter. It is never a good idea to breed those that belong to the same family. When you let this happen, there are chances of transmitting or acquiring genetic flaws. If your hamsters are healthy, you must make sure that they are not inbred at all times. It is not when you have a sick hamster that these genetic conditions are passed on. It happens especially with good hamsters that seem extremely healthy.

You can either adopt unrelated hamsters or can buy them. Adopting from someone who is also breeding them for a hobby is a great idea. Make sure you ask questions about the genetic line of the hamsters and their background is fully known to you. In a pet store or a breeder's, you are likely to find more information about this. With hamsters from a shelter, you can never be sure of the lineage and the possible genetic conditions of the hamster.

a. Sexing the hamster
You must be able to tell if your hamster is a male or a female. They look the same and it can be difficult to tell with hamsters. If you are buying them from a pet store or breeder, you should be sure that you are getting the right hamster for yourself.

In the case of Teddy Bear Hamsters, you will have an issue, as they are very difficult to assess until the age of four weeks. Until then, they are too small to tell the difference and you will also be unable to see the testicles of the male hamster.

Now, when you look at the rear end of the hamster you should be able to see two openings. One is the anus and the other is the reproductive organ of the hamster. If they are placed close to each other, then you have a female. If these openings are far away, almost as far as 2 cm, then it is a male hamster. This distinction is crucial to understand in order to prevent issues like territorial aggression in the same gender.

The next step is to make sure that the male and the female have their own space to live in. Remember, Teddy Bear Hamsters should never be put in one cage immediately. In fact, they should not be in the same cage until they are in heat.

Make sure that the cages provide the hamsters with a lot of exercise so that they can be physically and mentally active. That way, the chances of getting a healthy litter are higher.

In the cage of the female, provide additional bedding and nesting material that will make her instinctively ready to breed. If the hamster feels like the nesting material will not support her young, she may never go into heat and may never allow you to breed her for a new litter.

3. Introducing the male and female hamsters
Hamsters are ready to breed when they are about 10 weeks old. They can continue to breed until they are 15 months old. It is best to pair 1 male and 1 female as opposed to 1 male and multiple females as the case with other breeds of hamsters. The Teddy Bear Hamster is a lot more territorial and can be difficult to introduce a mate to.

Whether you have a male or a female hamster, it is never advisable to just put them in one cage and expect them to mate. There is a proper method of introducing Teddy Bear Hamsters.

The first step is to purchase a mate for your hamster that is not related. Then, as mentioned above, put both the hamsters in separate cages. Remember not to get a wired cage, as the newborn hamsters will slip right through the opening of the cages. It is a good idea to get an aquarium or a fiberglass cage. Give them enough food and water and keep an eye on the female to see if she is in heat.

It may be a good idea to place the cages next to each other and observe how these hamsters react to one another. Usually, they will only sniff one another and will not respond much to the other hamster as long as they are not in the same cage.

The next step is to check if the female is in heat. This can be done by stroking the rump of the hamster's tail. If it becomes erect after stroking, it means that your hamster is in heat. Do not just put her into the male's cage immediately. Check this for a few days, at least a week, and if the reaction is the same each time, it means that she is in heat. This is when the hamsters are ready to mate.

Usually a female hamster will be in heat ever 4-7 days. That is when you will watch out for these signs:

- She stays close to the ground
- Her tail is raised
- Her fur is smellier, as she is letting out pheromones

Carefully place the hamsters in the same cage. Remember, the female will not be placed in the cage of the male. You will have to do it vice versa, as the females are more aggressive in case of the Teddy Bear Hamsters.

Watch the response of the hamsters carefully. If there is any sign of aggression, separate them instantly. Even when the male mounts the female, she will get aggressive at times. The male will mount her and if she allows it, you can be certain that you will soon have a litter of puppies. With Teddy Bear Hamsters, the litter can be as large as 20 puppies each time.

Separate them after they have mated and put them back in their individual cages. It is a good idea to note down the date of mating so you know for sure how much time each pregnancy takes.

You will also have to maintain a record of the food you give the female hamster, her behavior after mating, her health or any other important details. Being organized with your data is the first step to ensuring that you have a healthy litter each time. You can even consult your vet for tips and gather advice about the methods that you have used for breeding.

4. Waiting for the puppies

As soon as the mating is over, isolating the female hamster is a great idea. In very rare cases, the male hamster will care for the puppies, but most often than not, they will eat or attack them. In the case of Syrian hamsters, even the gentlest pet can be extremely territorial and aggressive.

Now, what you really have to do is watch the progress of your female hamster. If she is pregnant, you will see the signs in some time. During this time, it is best that you avoid handling the hamster and you must just let her be.

By the time she is ready to have the babies you will see that the sides have very obvious saddlebags on either side. This is when you need to watch out for signs that tell you that she is ready to give birth:

- The hamster becomes extremely restless. She begins to pace around.

- The biggest sign is that she will start gathering food and will round up all the nesting material.

- After this, she will begin to give birth. You will see the sides of the hamster heaving as the bodies of the puppies emerge.

- She will deliver them on the move and will then pick them up herself in her mouth and take them back to the nest that she has built.

- What you must avoid is trying to help your hamster. If this is the first birth, it will look extremely in pain and uncomfortable. Nevertheless, do not interfere with your hamster and just let the birth happen naturally.

Here are some Do's and Don'ts for pregnant hamsters:

Do's:
- Provide them with a lot of bedding material
- Take your hamster to the vet to get a good prenatal test
- Make sure that you feed the mother well and give her supplements as prescribed by the vet
- The hamster requires a lot of water during this period.

Don'ts:
- Never stress out the female hamster

- Keep her in an area that is free from the reach of people, pets and children
- Do not interfere with the hamster and her puppies for at least one week after birth at any cost
- Make sure your hamster puppies do not get any solid food until they are at least 10 days old.

5. Caring for the puppies

If you have to raise baby hamsters, it is not really too much work if the mother is around. She will do most of the work related to the hamsters. All you need to make sure is that she has the environment that is required for her to take good care of her puppies. If you can ensure that there is enough food and nesting material, your puppies should be fine.

When the babies are just born, they are entirely dependent on the mother for all the care. They are born deaf, blind and without any fur. Now, a Teddy Bear Hamster will normally deliver about 20 puppies. However, she will only keep the number that she knows she can raise. The weakest puppies will either be eaten or killed. You do not have to feel bad about this and interfere, as it is the course of nature.

The puppies are covered with skin-like membrane that is called caul. Usually, each puppy is singly born and will be scattered all over the cage initially. This is also something that mom will take care of. She will bring them all to the nest after she has recovered herself. One thing you have to remember is that the caul will be eaten by the mother after birth. This is a nutritional requirement. You should not stop your hamster from doing this.

Make sure that you do not disturb this nest. If you notice that one of them has gotten out of the nest or is astray, the mother will take care of it. With hamsters, defense means that she will eat the puppy or kill it. If she sees any danger, she would rather mercifully kill the puppy than let them be in danger. Similarly, if she feels that her young ones will not have enough food or water, she is going to eat them. She will not let her puppies starve and would rather have them mercifully killed.

There may be instances when there is a spill or water leak in the hamster cage. Teddy Bear Hamster mothers are extremely persistent. They will make sure that all the puppies are immediately rehomed to the driest area of the nest.

You will have to scoop out all the wet bedding and replace it. If you feel like the area that the puppies have been moved to is dry, there is no need to disturb the nest.

However, if the nest is wet, you will have to remove the puppies and the mother from the cage. You can put the mother in a tiny bucket and all the puppies in a bowl. Remove all the accessories from the cage and wipe them dry. Then scoop out any area that is wet or soiled. Make sure you add a lot of nesting material for the mom to rebuild her nest. Put all the accessories back in the cage almost exactly like they were before to tell mom that you have not tampered with her cage.

Place the pups in the cage first in roughly the same place that they were in. The mom will most likely be very impatient. So, to comfort her, place a treat in the cage and put her next to this treat. Once the mom is back in the cage, you will not disturb them anymore. You can simply walk away and let the mom understand that you have helped her and the pups.

What you can do to help the puppies is lower the level of water so that they are able to drink on their own when they are ready to explore the cage. It is only around the seventh or eighth day that they begin to look like hamsters. The fur grows and they have very obvious markings on their body, but they are still unable to see. You will notice some developmental changes in them. They will be able to hold food while they nibble, for instance.

When you notice that the eyes of your hamsters are opening, understand that the cage requires a good cleaning. This is when you can safely handle the puppies. You will need to thoroughly clean the cage even after the puppies have been weaned.

Ideally, weaning should be done between 21 to 28 days after the birth of the puppies. That is when they are ready to leave their mother. You must check the gender of the hamster puppies and make sure that they are kept in separate cages. The only thing you need to do is ensure that hamsters that are too tiny or have very little chances of survival are left with the mother for a week or two more. When they look healthy, you can get them out of the cage and into their separate cage.

Now, you can think of putting up ads if you want to give your hamsters away or introduce them to people who have offered to take them home as pets. If you plan to raise them in your home, you will have to make sure that they are housed individually as they are not going to be able to stay safely together for too long.

6. Caring for orphaned puppies

In some unfortunate cases, the mother hamster will not be able to make it through the birth of the puppies. If she dies or abandons the litter, then the onus is on you to take care of the puppies until they are ready to be weaned. Hamster puppies are extremely small and delicate and you need to be immensely careful if you want to take care of them without hurting them.

a. 12-14 days of age

If your hamster puppies are about 12 to 14 days old, you have a lot of hope when it comes to saving their lives. Here are the steps that you want to follow:

- Make sure you clean the cage thoroughly after the mom has passed on. Keep the babies in a small bowl while you do this.

- Put a lot of bedding into the cage. The best option for young hamsters is tissue paper shreds, as they are not only warm but also extremely safe and soft for the babies.

- It is a good idea to put the cage in a warm location in your house. There should be no drafts in the area that you are placing the cage in. If you feel like the puppies are cold, you will have to place a heating pad on a low heat just below the cage. The job of the mom hamster is to provide the heat required for the babies. This is why you will see her sleeping with them at all times.

- You need to lower the water bottle level so that the puppies can drink it easily. It may help to add some Pedialite that is unflavored to ensure that they do not get dehydrated.

- The food dish should contain a lot of seed and grain mix that you can also sprinkle with some milk powder. Quick oats and wheat germ are also a good idea, provided that you soak it in water and make it easy for the puppies to eat.

- Adding some additional protein to this can also help. Mashed canned dog food or even some boiled egg can be placed in a separate saucer.

- To keep them hydrated, it is a good idea to provide them with some apple as well. Balancing the diet of the puppies is crucial. You do not have to provide them with any treats at this point.

- If you have not found the body of the mother hamster, it may even mean that she has taken a small vacation to cool off and relax. That is when you should refrain from washing the cage so that the mother hamster can find her way back with the scent.

- When you suspect that the mother hamster has taken off, you can even place some live traps around the house or use the same techniques as mentioned in the previous chapters about finding your hamster.

b. Below 10 days of age

In case your hamster puppies are less than 10 years of age, it is a good idea to adopt a female who can provide mother's milk to the babies. That is the best option to ensure survival. You may contact local breeders to help you out with this process. Once you have found options, here are a few things that you may consider:

- Get the puppies warm. They will be undoubtedly very cold when you find them. Wrap the puppies in a clean and dry towel.

- Let the blood start circulating properly. For this you will have to rub the body of the babies gently.

- When you remove the babies from the nest, make sure you clean up all of the residue from it. Do not remove the whole nesting material.

- The adoptive mother would ideally be one that has already had a litter that is about 2-3 days old.

- You will have to place some of the nesting material from the adopted mother's nest and place it around the nest of the orphaned puppies to help with the scent.

- Take some of the nesting material and hold each puppy in it and allow them to wiggle around in it for a while. That way, they will have the scent of the adopted mother's puppies.

- You will have to place the puppies in the cage of the adopted mother.

- First distract the mother with a treat. Following that, place the orphans among her babies. Hopefully, the scent will blend in.

- After you have done this, leave the nest alone and don't even take a peek for about a week.

This is one of the most successful methods but is not entirely fool proof. The success of your attempt lies in the hands of the mother hamster. If she notices that something is amiss, then she will dispose the puppies as an act of mercy.

If you are lucky, however, she will not notice the difference and will probably take good care of the new babies as well. With hamsters, they will not notice an increase or decrease in the size of the litter. They only rely on scent. Teddy Bear Hamsters and all other types of Syrian hamsters have been known to be most successful with adoption.

c. If adoption is not possible
In some cases, it may be difficult to find a mother who will adopt the orphaned puppies. You may not have access to a breeder or there may not be any hamster that has recently given birth. In those cases, these are the steps that you can follow to increase the chances of survival of the litter:

- You will have to feed the puppies around the clock. You can use an eyedropper to feed the puppies. They will have to be fed every one hour when they are less than 12 days old and about every 3 hours when they are older. This will have to continue until they reach the weaning age, which is about 21 days.

- For the actual feed, you can give your puppies kitten milk replacer. If not, you can even give them baby formula. Evaporated milk that is 50% reduced can also be given after mixing it with an equal portion of warm water.

- You will have to give them three drops every hour. When they are ready for solid food, you can reduce the quantity to about 5ml in each feed.

- After each feed, it is necessary to stimulate the puppies to defecate and urinate. The mother hamster will actually do this for them. When you are raising the puppies, take a moist and warm cloth and rub the anal and genital area with it.

- It is also possible that the puppies will dehydrate very easily. When they start eating dry food or solid food, placing a piece of apple without the peel is a great way to prevent any chances of dehydration. If the puppies are able to drink from the bottle, add some Pedialite in it. This reduces dehydration to a large extent.

It is up to us to hope that the puppies will survive without the mother. The one thing you have to ensure is that the food that you give them is not forced into their mouths. You have to be extra careful when you are feeding them with the eyedropper. If you force the liquid in, there are chances that the puppy will inhale it and if it gets to the lungs, they will not survive.

In a home set up, it is quite unlikely that the puppies will be abandoned by the mother. However, if that were to happen, you need to make sure that you are prepared to prevent the death of an entire litter. Hand feeding them is a lot of work but it will be worth all the effort.

Chapter 8: Hamster Health

The size of a hamster makes it very important to pay attention to any chances of injury or illness in the animal. Even the smallest health issue can become very complex if not treated well.

The issue with hamsters is that you will most likely not even notice that he has a health issue. They will hide the symptoms for a rather long time. Keeping an eye on their eating habits or any change in the regular routine of your hamster can really help you understand his health.

If see that there could be a problem with your pet, consult your vet immediately for assistance. Even if it is a false alarm, you have to understand that prevention is always better than cure, especially with an animal as small as a hamster. Here are some of the sure shot signs of a hamster that is unwell:

- He becomes very inactive
- You will always find him huddled up in a corner
- There will be a significant loss of appetite
- He will seem unkempt.
- He sneezes quite often
- You will notice liquid oozing from the nose and the eyes
- He may show signs of wheezing
- There will be significant wetness near the tail region
- You will notice diarrhea
- Hair loss is very prominent in the hamster
- His back will be humped.

The best way to prevent any illness in your hamster is to make sure that you keep him well groomed and also take good care of the cage. If the hamster is kept in unhygienic surroundings, he will feel extremely stressed. You must also make sure that he is not stressed by a pet or any other source in your house. That will make him more prone to infections and deadly diseases.

1. Common illnesses with hamsters

Hamsters are prone to infections and problems. However, there are some illnesses that are common in hamsters. In this section we will talk about all the health issues faced by hamsters:

a. Heart disorders

It is very common for hamsters to develop blood clots in their heart, especially in the upper chamber. This condition is known as atrial thrombosis and can be detrimental to the hamster's health. You will see that all the blockages are usually on the left side of the heart.

Congestive heart failure

This is when the heart of the hamster becomes extremely weak and is simply unable to pump any blood. The condition is more common in older hamsters and is usually associated with a secondary condition called amyloidosis.

Symptoms:

- Shortness of breath
- Irregularity in the heartbeat
- A blue tinge on the skin

Treatment:
There is no definitive treatment for this condition. However, you will be able to manage the condition effectively with the right medication. The best thing to do is to prevent the condition with measures like a good diet, proper exercise and a healthy environment for the hamster to thrive in. That will keep the heart healthy.

b. Digestive issues

The digestive system of a hamster is quite sensitive. They are prone to developing a lot of conditions if they have not been raised in a good environment. Some of the most common digestive disorders are:

Proliferative enteritis

This is a type of inflammation that will spread all over the small intestine of the hamster. This leads to diarrhea.

Cause:

This condition is transmitted by bacteria called *Lawsonia Intracellularis.* This tends to infect the hamster if:

- He is not transported correctly
- The cage is overcrowded
- He has had some illness or surgery in the past
- His diet has been changed recently.

This condition is mostly seen in younger hamsters. There is very little time for diagnosis, as the condition spreads rather fast, making the hamster really sick, really fast.

Symptoms:
- The belly and the tail become wet and look matted
- The energy levels are very low
- You will see that he loses his appetite
- Rapid weight loss is also another issue with diarrhea.

Diagnosis for this condition is usually done with the help of the history of the animal and the symptoms of the condition that he is suffering from.

Treatment:
- Antibiotics that are added to the water
- Fluids are given to the hamster through injections or orally

Preventive measures:
- Keep any infected hamster away from the healthy animals in your home
- Clean the cage of the infected hamster thoroughly
- Make sure that his cage is sanitized regularly.

Tyzzer's disease
This is another digestive disorder with symptoms very similar to proliferative enteritis. This is a disorder that is very common with hamsters that are stressed or much younger. If you have another hamster at home and keep the cage of your Teddy Bear Hamster close to him, you need to make sure that they are separated in order to prevent the spreading of this disease. The bacterium that causes this disorder forms spores. Therefore, the disease can even spread to other pets or hamsters in your home. As a preventive measure you need to sanitize all the water and food containers used by the healthy animals in your home as well as the unwell ones.

Causes:
This condition is caused by bacteria called *Clostridium piliforme*. If there are any feces that contain this bacterium, your hamster can consume it and contract the condition. Therefore, it is extremely important to keep the cage clean. Stress is another important factor that causes this condition in hamsters.

It is also possible that the small intestines are inflamed by the use of antibiotics. There are certain antibiotics that are known as gram-positive antibiotics. They can be fatal to your hamster. Once these antibiotics are consumed, the symbiotic bacteria that live in the intestines are killed and the harmful bacteria become prominent. This makes the pouch just behind the intestines inflamed, leading to profuse bleeding.

The condition can be diagnosed based on the medication that the pet has received. One possible cure for this condition is actually consuming the feces of a healthy hamster to reinstate the level of the useful bacteria in the hamster's intestines.

Symptoms:
- Dehydration
- Watery stools
- Complete loss of appetite
- Sudden death.

Salmonellosis
This condition results from the inflammation of the intestines, which again has very similar symptoms to diarrhea.

Causes:
This condition is caused by a strain of bacteria called *Salmonella*. It is not really common in hamsters.

Prevention and Treatment:
You will follow the same measures as the treatment for proliferative enteritis in the case of these animals.

Protozoa
These are single celled animals that can upset the digestive tract of a hamster. You will notice that the digestive tracts of healthy hamsters have some traces of protozoa. However, if your hamster gets stressed or is young, these protozoans can cause infections. As a result, the hamster will have diarrhea.

A vet will be able to diagnose this condition by checking the feces of the hamster. Adding metronidazole to the water of your pet is the best solution to this condition.

Tapeworms

These parasites are more common in hamsters in comparison to other rodents like mice or rats. You will not see any signs in an infected hamster. If the infection is very serious, the intestine will get inflamed and the intestine will be blocked. In the worst cases the lymph nodes will also get infected. Treatment is very similar to that of any form of diarrhea except in the case of severe infection.

Constipation
It is possible for hamsters to become constipated if they have developed any parasite in their digestive tract. This condition is normally contracted when they eat any portion of their bedding. That is when the intestine may get blocked, leading to a fold in a part of the intestine. This condition is also known as intussusception.

This condition can be caused when the intestines are inflamed. When the hamster does not get enough water or has a poor diet, this condition occurs. It may also occur during pregnancy. The hamster has a protrusion in the anus, which is tubular in shape.

When this condition occurs it is usually considered a medical emergency. You will have to consult your vet immediately and will have to surgically have the protrusion removed. If you do not attend to this condition instantly, it can be fatal. Even when surgery is immediate, there is no chance of immediate recovery for the hamster.

You will have to identify the cause of the condition first. You may have to surgically have a section of the intestines removed and two portions of the intestine will need some sort of bypass that is connected.

Actinomycosis
This is another type of infection that is normally caused by a fungus called Actinomyces bovis. This is also a rare condition in hamsters. The dangers of this condition include rupturing of the salivary glands. You may see that a lot of pus oozes from these ruptured glands. If your vet is able to diagnose the condition with a test in the lab, your hamster can be treated.

The infected area is lanced and drained. This is followed by a prescription of necessary antibiotics.

Cholangiofibrosis
This condition is also called liver scarring. When the older hamsters have to deal with inflammation and degeneration of the liver, it will cause inflammation. You will see in the blood tests that the liver is producing an

increased number of hormones. However, the cause of this condition is not fully known and therefore you do not have any effective treatment for this condition either. This condition is particularly common in females.

c. Eye and Ear issues
Needless to say, the eyes and ears of a hamster are extremely sensitive. There are a few infections and disorders that you need to watch out for. The most common eye and ear issues are:

Conjunctivitis

Also known as pink eye, this condition affects hamsters just the way it affects human beings. You will see an inflammation of the eye and also swelling of the entire face of the hamster.

Causes:

- Bacterial infection
- Dust in the bedding
- Bite wounds

Treatment:
- Remove any crusted material from the eye of the hamster
- The vet will flush the eye with a special solution
- You can use a prescribed ointment to make the healing process faster.

Eyeball protrusion
This is a rather common condition in a hamster.

Causes:
- Eye infection
- Trauma
- Tight restraint pulling on the skin on the back of the neck

This condition should be treated instantly in order to help save the eye of the hamster. It is a medical emergency that requires immediate attention to make sure that it is solved on time. You cannot do anything but take your hamster to the vet immediately when you notice this condition in your pet.

d. Muscle, bone and joint disorders
Any strain in the tendon or the muscle of the hamster can make him unable to walk properly. The most common issue with hamsters is broken bones.

Causes:

- The leg getting stuck in a laddered wheel
- The limb getting stuck in the wired cage
- Any loose threads or fibers entangling the leg of the hamster
- Jumping off a surface that is at a height
- Someone stepping on him accidentally
- A scuffle with your pet.

Symptoms:
- Your hamster is not able to move
- He is reluctant to make movements of any kind, even towards food
- An otherwise friendly hamster is refusing to be picked up
- He will drag one foot.

Treatment:
The first thing you will have to do is take the hamster to a vet. The vet will put a splint on his leg and wrap it up.

If there are any prescribed anti-inflammatory medicines or pain medicines that the vet recommends, make sure that you administer it as asked.

During this time, any ladders, wheels or toys that are in the cage should be removed. Even the tunnels should be blocked.

There should be absolutely no strain on the hamster. It is also a good idea to put the hamster in an aquarium when required. That way, there is no chance of getting stressed out by climbing wires and bars. You must lower the water bottle to make sure that the hamster is able to drink water easily.

It should take about 2 weeks for your hamster to heal if the break is just mild. However, with a severe injury where the bone is out of the skin, it will take longer. In these cases, hamsters tend to chew off their bones.

Any complication in the healing process must be reported to the vet. Infection is the only thing that you need to be concerned about when your hamster has an injury.

There are chances that your hamster will have a limp permanently. However, that should not affect his health in the long term.

e. Nutritional disorders
With hamsters, the maximum amount of nutritional diseases occurs when the hamster is about to deliver a litter. Usually, a lack of vitamin E is very common in pregnant hamsters. That is when the offspring will either be

stillborn or weak. It is also possible that a lack of nutrients will drive the hamster to eat her offspring.

The vet will be able to see swelling or bleeding in the skull or spine, which is a clear indication that the hamster is deprived of Vitamin E.

In other cases when the hamster, male or young female, has a deficiency it will lead to a lot of muscular disorders and may cause weakness. In extreme cases, it may even paralyze the hamster. You will have to check with your vet if you are not sure about the amount of vitamin E that is required in the diet of your hamster. There are several natural food sources that can help your hamster too.

f. Airway and lung problems
Since the hamster is so small in its size, any disorder of the airway or the lung can become serious very soon. Here are some signs that there is some lung or airway-related problem with your hamster:

- He is having a lot of trouble breathing
- He is wheezing
- You can hear a strange noise when he breathes.

There are a few conditions that are quite common in hamsters. If you notice any of the mentioned symptoms, contact your vet immediately.

Pneumonia

This inflammation of the lungs is not very common in hamsters. However, if it does occur, it is because of some sort of infection. There are several kinds of bacteria and viruses that can cause this infection. There is no singular causal factor for infection.

It is common for these bacteria to be present in the digestive system or the respiratory system of the animal. It is seen in very small numbers. These organisms multiply quickly, causing serious infections.

Causes:

- Sudden change in temperature
- Deviation from the normal environment
- Stressful situations.

Symptoms:
- Significant loss in appetite
- Lack of activity
- Extreme difficulty breathing

Treatment:
In most cases, it is believed that treatment is not effective for pneumonia in hamsters. Antibiotics can be administered if the case is mild.

In addition to all this, you can make your hamster feel less stressed by providing him with a clean cage that is dry and warm, reducing any stressors in his environment and also injecting fluids. If there are any hamsters around your Teddy Bear Hamster, albeit in a separate cage, make sure you get them away to prevent any infection from spreading to your beloved pets. Even other household pets are at the risk of contracting serious issues.

Para influenza
This is another rare health issue in hamsters that is caused by the *Sendai virus*. This condition usually spreads from one hamster to the other. Even if you have two separate cages that are placed close to one another, this disease can spread by simple sneezing or even coughing.

This condition is rare but when it does occur, it is highly contagious.

Symptoms:
• Sneezing
• Coughing
• Dripping from the nose
• Oozing from the nose
• Troubled breathing
• Pneumonia.

This condition leads to death if neglected. You will not see these signs in adult hamsters and they may just succumb. It is most likely that a newborn hamster will exhibit these signs. There are also several chances of a secondary bacterial infection when you neglect the condition.

Treatment:
• Fluids are provided under the skin
• Food supplements
• Antibiotics for bacterial infection.

Although this type of viral condition does not have any complete cure, it can be managed quite well.

g. Reproductive disorders

Female hamsters that are breeding will develop several reproductive disorders. The most common problems with these hamsters are:

- Infertility due to old age
- Small litters
- Malnutrition
- Abnormal estrous cycle.

There are several factors like the temperature, availability of light, the season and other small factors that play a crucial role in the reproductive ability of your hamster.

Many times the hamster fetus will die in the womb. Cannibalism is quite prominent in hamsters and they tend to chew up their own young. However, this behavior is only seen when the hamster has been given a poor diet, is handled a lot, has a male hamster in the same cage after giving birth, does not have ample nesting material, is not able to produce milk, the offspring are deformed or unwell or the milk glands are inflamed.

Mammary gland infection

This is a condition that is caused by a strain of bacteria called *Streptococcus*. You will see that the infection manifests about 10 days after the birth of a litter.

The glands that are affected by the condition will appear swollen and will also discharge a lot of mucus and pus. The mother will eat the young because of this condition, as she is unable to provide the nutritional requirements for the little ones. The cause of the infection can be determined using simple tests and can even be treated using an antibiotic.

h. Skin disorders

Skin problems are the most common ones in the case of hamsters. They suffer from infections that are either caused by parasites or by other microbes. It is necessary to keep a check on the fur and the skin of your hamster. Any hair loss is a sign that there is a serious problem.

Skin abscesses

These are pockets of pus just under the skin that are caused by an infection. The most common cause of skin abscesses is an injury caused by a sharp object that is in the cage.

You will notice that often, the abscesses are on the head of the hamster.

Symptoms:

- The lymph nodes around the neck area are swollen
- The cheek pouches seem to be infected
- In the case of male hamsters, there are certain glands just over the hip that get infected
- There could be injuries on the shoulder or feet that can get infected.

Treatment:
You can drain the abscesses and apply antibiotics to them. If the abscesses have burst on their own, you can have them cleaned and get some antibiotics applied to them. It is necessary to apply an antibiotic ointment regularly on the hamster's wounds.

It is possible to have these abscesses removed with a simple surgical procedure. In the case of an infection of the flanks, it may become necessary to even clean the area around it. In these cases, steroids are very important for the hamster.

To prevent any more abscesses, you need to make sure that there are no sharp edges in the cage. You should also avoid any wood shavings inside the cage.

Hair loss
This condition is also called alopecia. This is when large tufts of hair fall off the body of the hamster.

Causes:
- The body of the hamster rubbing constantly against the cage
- The nutrition is not good enough for the hamster
- A form of T-cell lymphoma or cancer
- Infestation with parasites and mites
- An imbalance in the thyroid glands
- Problems with the functioning of the kidney
- Formation of any tumor in the adrenal glands.

Treatment will be determined by the causal factor of this condition entirely.

Ringworm
The name is often misconstrued. Ringworm is a disease caused by a fungal infection and not a worm of any sort. The skin is infected by a fungus that

usually thrives in an unclean and damp environment. So, if you are not cleaning the cage often, this issue may occur.

This type of skin infection is mostly the result of fungi that belong to the *Microsporum and Tricophyton* species.

Symptoms:
- Bald patches
- Crusts and flakes on the edges of these patches
- Redness of the skin.

Causes:
- Improper sanitation
- Passed on infection from human beings
- Too much time outside the cage.

Treatment:
A special lamp is used to examine these spots. In order to treat this condition, an antifungal ointment is used. You can even use a scrub that is specially made with iodine. The vet may also administer a certain type of medicine that is known as griseoffluvin that is orally administered. This is a contagious disease, so if you are cleaning the cage of your infected hamster, be sure to wear gloves. Use them even when you handle the hamster. It is a good idea to also wash your hands well, even if you are using gloves.

Mite infection
Hamsters are most prone to infections by mites. They will develop fur and skin infections. The most common species of mites that will infect a hamster are *Demodex aurati and Demodex criceti.*

The condition is very common in male hamsters and older hamsters. This is because these groups are likely to develop issues related to malnutrition.

Symptoms:
- Inflammation of the skin
- Dry and scaly skin
- Hair loss
- Bald patches
- Dry and scaly patches that do not itch.

Treatment:

The body is washed with a special shampoo that has a healing ingredient called selenium sulfide. You can also use an ointment that contains amitraz.

There are other species of mites that can infect a hamster. The ones that are least common are nose mites, ear mites and also rat mites. If your hamster is infected by any of these mites, you will see localized inflammation of the skin.

In cases of the lesser-known mite infections, a medicine called ivermectin is prescribed. You will have to change the bedding of the hamster on a regular basis to make sure that it is safe to use.

i. Kidney disorders
Any inflammation of the kidney can be a concern for older hamsters, particularly the females.

Causes:

- Disorder in the immune system
- Extremely high blood pressure in the kidney
- Viral infections.

Symptoms:

- Drastic weight loss
- More urination
- Unusual thirst.

j. Multiple organ disorders
There are a few conditions that can affect different systems of the body. These conditions are also known as systemic diseases.

Arenavirus infection
This is a strain of virus that normally affects wild mice. The condition is also known as Lymphocytic Choriomeningitis virus infection.

Causes:
- Any contact with the urine or saliva of wild mice
- Droplets expelled into the air by another infected hamster
- The mother hamster is infected.

In most cases, the hamster will recover on its own. It is humans who are in danger of catching an infection.

Symptoms:
- Sudden weight loss
- Depression
- Reduced reproduction
- Depression
- Swollen lymph nodes
- Enlargement of the kidney, spleen or liver.

It is best that an animal with this condition is euthanized. He is likely to spread the disease to you. People who have been diagnosed with this infection will have inflammation in the brain membrane and the spinal cord. The symptoms are very similar to flu.

If you have a hamster with this condition, here are a few precautionary measures that you can take:
- Clean the cage with gloves on, especially when you are handling urine or feces
- Use disposable gloves and make sure you dispose of the contents of the cage carefully
- Wash your hands all the way up to the arms
- Any clothing that might accidentally come intp contact with the bedding or any item in the cage should be washed immediately.

Amyloidosis
Several sheets of a type of dense protein named amyloids are created when the hamster develops this condition. This protein will build up in many organs such as the kidneys and the liver. Eventually, the normal functioning of the organ is compromised.

The condition is very common in hamsters that are over a year old. It is also seen in hamsters that have had illnesses for a long period of time. It is very common for a female hamster to be infected.

You will not notice this condition until the functioning of the kidney or liver has started to deteriorate. The most common symptoms are:
- Rough hair
- Loss of appetite
- Depression
- Fluid accumulation in the body
- A hunched posture
- Fluid accumulation in the body
- Depression.

This is not a condition that can be treated. The only thing you can possibly do is keep the hamster comfortable with several fluids. If your hamster develops this condition, he will not live too long.

Polycystic disease
This is a disease that leads to cysts. Fluid-filled sacs are very common in hamsters that are about a year old. The sacs normally develop in the liver. They are usually less than 3 centimeters in diameter.

There are several other sex glands like the pancreas, ovaries and the accessory sexual glands that can get infected by this condition.

Pseudotuberculosis
This condition is caused by a strain of bacteria called *Yersinia pseudotuberulosis*. This is a serious infection in hamsters that can poison the blood.

Causes:
• Coming into contact with the feces of rodents and wild birds.

Symptoms:
• Weight loss
• Diarrhea
• Degeneration of multiple organs including the spleen, gall bladder, lungs, walls of the intestines and the liver.

This is another condition that is contagious to pet owners. Since there is no treatment for this condition, it is highly recommended that the hamster that has come into contact with this condition be euthanized immediately. You will have to sanitize and clean the cage of the sick hamster immediately. Gloves and other bedding material must be disposed of to make sure that you do not catch the infection. It is also important to wash up really well after you are done.

Tularemia
This is a condition that is quite rare in hamsters. But when it occurs, it will lead to very severe illness, blood poisoning and even death.

This condition is caused in hamsters by mite or tick infection. If your hamster suddenly develops roughness in his coat, there are chances that he has been infected. If he develops this condition, he will die within 48 hours.

What you need to remember is that this condition, too, is contagious. The best option is to euthanize a hamster that has been infected. Following that, his cage and all the contents should be sanitized. Wear gloves when you do this and remember to dispose of the gloves and the bedding in a sealed bag. After that, your hands must be thoroughly washed and cleaned.

k. Cancer

Tumors and cancers are not very common in hamsters. There is only a 4% chance that your hamster will develop this condition. There are several environmental and genetic factors that contribute to the development of this condition.

Some tumors are not cancerous and are very common in the areas that digest the food or produce hormones. There are environmental and genetic factors that contribute to the formation of tumors.

It is common for older hamsters to develop lymphomas. These are basically tumors of the lymph nodes, spleen, liver, thymus and similar sites.

Symptoms:

- Fatigue
- Patchy baldness
- Inflammation of the skin
- Weight loss.

It is also possible that the womb, eyes, hair follicles and the brain of the hamster will develop tumors. Be very attentive when you handle your hamster. If you notice the slightest lump or growth, speak to your vet immediately. If you detect a tumor early, it is a lot easier to treat and is the best option for your hamster.

2. Hamster first aid

There are some injuries that will require immediate attention and may not even require any visit to the vet. You need to be able to identify when you can help the hamster at home and when you really need the assistance of a vet.

a. When can you treat him at home?

If your hamster only has small bites and cuts or even commonly known parasites, it is not necessary to approach a vet.

b. When do you need to go to a vet?

If any wound is serious, visit the vet immediately. Because of their small bodies, these creatures do not have too much blood in them. So even with the smallest negligence they can lose a lot of blood. If your pet is showing signs of troubled breathing or is making rasping noises, make sure you see a vet.

c. Preparing a hamster first aid kit

It is good to have a hamster first aid kit handy. Make sure that you have all of the following to deal with major and minor issues easily.

- Clean towel
- Large clean towel
- 3 percent hydrogen peroxide
- Q-tips
- Triple Antibiotic topical solution or ointment
- 10 cc syringes without the needles
- Tweezers
- Gauze
- Heating Pad
- Cage for isolation
- Travel cage

d. How to treat minor bites and cuts

There are chances that your hamster may bite you if he is in pain, so make sure that he is restrained with a clean towel wrapped around him. Syringes should be used to clean the wound and flush them. Use saline solution and pat the area dry with a sterile piece of gauze.

The wound should then be disinfected with an antiseptic solution. Pat it dry and apply the antibiotic ointment.

It is best that you keep the animal in an isolated cage when he is being treated. Keep this cage boring so that the hamster will be able to get more rest and will sleep more. You can take him back to his original cage after he has recovered. Make sure that you monitor the food and water consumption of your pet after this injury. If the routine changes drastically, see a vet immediately.

You need to make sure that you assess the cause of this injury. If it is because of a household pet, make sure that your hamster cage is out of reach to prevent this from occurring.

If that is not the source of the injury, inspect the environment of your hamster and ensure that it is not because of a toy, a sharp edge in the cage or some loose wire. It could also be because of poorly groomed nails.

e. First aid for major bleeding

The first thing to do would be to apply pressure on the wound with a towel or some gauze. Then rush your pet to the vet, as you do not want your pet bleeding to death. It is also a good idea to place him in a travel cage to prevent further injury due to struggling. You must not even attempt to clean major wounds yourself, as you will put the animal at a great risk.

Conclusion

The main purpose of this book is to ensure that hamster owners are more responsible with their pet and understand the seriousness of owning a small animal.

These animals require constant care, too. Unless you know how to take good care of them, you are putting their life at risk. These creatures are small and are therefore a lot more delicate to handle. It is important that you keep your knowledge about your pet updated at all times.

Here's hoping that you were able to find all the information that you require about caring for your hamster. It is also important that this book is able to help those considering the option of buying a pet hamster for themselves make that decision.

Here's wishing you a fun-filled journey with your little pet. Undoubtedly, you have a great companion who will keep you happy and, of course, entertained.

References

From time to time, it is a great idea to upgrade your knowledge about hamsters. There may be new trends and ideas that can help you improve the quality of life of your pet. Now, what better place to look in than the Internet. Here are a few websites that you can certainly find great, practical advice on.

Note: at the time of printing, all the websites below were working. As the Internet changes rapidly, some sites might no longer be live when you read this book. That is, of course, out of our control.

www.hamster-club.com/
www.theanimalfiles.com/
www.hamsterific.com/
www.merckvetmanual.com/
www.animals.mom.me/
www.pets.stackexchange.com/
www.hamsterhideout.com
www.midwestexotichospital.com
www.petcha.com
www.purrsngrrs.com
www.caringpets.org
www.theanimalfiles.com
www.thehamsterhouse.com
www.hamsters-uk.org
www.pethamstercare.com
www.pethelpful.com
www.exoticpets.about.com
www.oureverydaylife.com
www.hamstersaspets.co.uk
www.humanesociety.org
www.choosehamstercages.com
www.thehamsterplace.com
www.voices.nationalgeographic.com
www.southernhamsterclub.co.uk
www.hamsterfanciers.com
www.petscorner.co.uk
www.petwebsite.com
www.hamstercentral.com
www.wamiz.co.uk
www.syrianhamster.tumblr.com
www.thehamsterblog.com

www.howtohamster.blogspot.com
www.syrianhamstercare.blogspot.com
https://piscespets.com
www.tinkyhamstery.blogspot.com
www.thatpetblog.com
www.blogs.evergreen.edu
www.hamsterfanaticforum.co.uk
www.hamstercagefinder.com
www.dwerghamster.nl

Published by IMB Publishing 2016

Made in the USA
Middletown, DE
21 December 2020